Hatred Pursued
Beyond the Grave

Hatred Pursued Beyond the Grave

Tales of our Ancestors
from the
London Church Courts

JANE COX

Published in association with
the Public Record Office

London: HMSO

Applications for reproduction should be made to HMSO Copyright Unit

ISBN 0 11 440239 6

British Library Cataloguing in Publication Data
A CIP catalogue record for this book
is available from the British Library

Design by HMSO

Cover: Detail from *Le Fils Maudit*, or *The Ungrateful Son*, by Jean Baptiste Greuze.
(Musée du Louvre, Paris/Bridgeman Art Library, London)

Published by HMSO and available from:

HMSO Publications Centre
(Mail, fax and telephone orders only)
PO Box 276, London, SW8 5DT
Telephone orders 0171 873 9090
General enquiries 0171 873 0011
(queuing system in operation for both numbers)
Fax orders 0171 873 8200

HMSO Bookshops
49 High Holborn, London, WC1V 6HB
(counter service only)
0171 873 0011 Fax 0171 831 1326
68–69 Bull Street, Birmingham, B4 6AD
0121 236 9696 Fax 0121 236 9699
33 Wine Street, Bristol, BS1 2BQ
0117 9264306 Fax 0117 9294515
9–21 Princess Street, Manchester, M60 8AS
0161 834 7201 Fax 0161 833 0634
16 Arthur Street, Belfast, BT1 4GD
01232 238451 Fax 01232 235401
71 Lothian Road, Edinburgh, EH3 9AZ
0131 228 4181 Fax 0131 229 2734
The HMSO Oriel Bookshop
The Friary, Cardiff CF1 4AA
01222 395548 Fax 01222 384347

HMSO's Accredited Agents
(see Yellow Pages)

and through good booksellers

Printed in the United Kingdom for HMSO
Dd 297935 C18 4/95 3396/2 20249

This book is dedicated to the memory of my aunt

ELFRIDA MARY CARTER

*who in a bleak post-war London conjured up
spirits from the pageant of English history to delight
a little girl's imagination.*

Contents

Preface

The records of the Church courts have been slow to take their place as significant source material for 'History, the Science'. Perhaps it is because they are difficult to read and understand and many of them have only fairly recently become accessible. Perhaps it is because they sound as if they might be tedious and unrewarding.

In the early 1960s there were brought to the Public Record Office from Somerset House 84 tons of records, the archive of the Prerogative Court of Canterbury, the archbishop's probate court.

The records are wills and the documentation of lawsuits over wills. They span 600 years, from the late fourteenth century to 1858, and comprise one of the single richest sources for social, economic and local history, genealogy and biography that has survived. The wills themselves have always been available for public search but the rest has not, and even though most of the new material has been catalogued, relatively little use has been made of it.

For ten years, armed with a vacuum cleaner and an industrial mask, I cleared the dust from the PCC (as it is known in the trade) archive. Gradually I became intimately acquainted with a fascinating world, one which did not, to my mind, conform with what I had read in published historical works. It is that world which I would like to share.

The PCC occupied the same premises as a host of other Church courts in a complex of buildings in the City of London known as Doctors' Commons. In order that the picture should not have an unrelieved black border, I have included some of the records of matrimonial and defamation suits from these other courts.

The defamation and probate suits have the lion's share. The latter for obvious reasons, and the former because it is very unusual to find any source material which allows the re-creation of the conversation of ordinary working folk, particularly women, from three or four hundred years ago.

The period covered is, at its extremities, from the sixteenth to the nineteenth century. Much of the material is from the Restoration period. I have concentrated on the seventeenth century because the records for those times are especially rich, and out of a simple partiality for and a familiarity with 'good King Charles's golden days'.

Most of the characters come from London, many from east London, and from the Home Counties. It is a turbulent, urban crew, brawling, drinking, loving and hating. The stories are of anger and bitterness, showing human nature in its worst light. Women feature at least as much as men, if not more, for reasons which will be explained, and ordinary people as much as lords and ladies. There are even some children.

It is an archivist's tale, with a minimum of quantifying and few conclusions drawn. All I ask is that you come with me through the twilight streets, before the curtains are drawn, and look into the homes of our ancestors.

Acknowledgements

For the material used in the chapters on marriage and scolds, I am grateful, in the approved fashion, to the splendid staff of the Guildhall Library and the Greater London Record Office, who are both charming and well informed.

I would like to thank Lady Bowes-Lyon and the Hon. Simon and Caroline Bowes-Lyon for letting me use the Countess of Strathmore's scrapbook, and Veronica Williamson for suggesting it.

Robert Latham, the editor of Pepys, and my supervisor at London University long ago, brushed up an enjoyment of Restoration London which my mother's devotion to Pepys had implanted, and gave me some genealogical information about the diarist's family.

For the probate part, there is much more to be said. Over the many years I spent with 84 tons of Prerogative Court of Canterbury (PCC) records, I received help from many dear colleagues at the Public Record Office who worked with me cataloguing the records. This book is theirs as much as mine. The cast and the parts each played are, very roughly, in order of appearance; if I have forgotten anybody, I am truly sorry. Their names and the records they worked on are: Margaret and the late Irvine Gray (a catalogue of over 50,000 inventories, a biographical list of officers of the PCC and deposition indexes), Carol Dimmer, Graham Attfield and Vanessa Carr (depositions), Charles Ross and Charles Gray (inventories), Sarah Lenton and Anne Layzell (inventories and cartoons), Peter Meldrum (sentences), Chris Kitching (inventories and early proceedings), Duncan Harrington, an expert on Kentish records who taught me much (bonds and commissions), Noel Whiteside (general rummaging), Geraldine Beech (depositions), Sue Lumas (unearthing the story of the Pinchbeck family), Norah Fuidge (depositions), Tim Groom (administrations), Michael Jubb (Milton), Eddie Higgs (death duty registers), Gervase Hood (everything that had still to be done).

I am most grateful to Sue Palmer, the Archivist at Sir John Soane's Museum, for giving me access to her records and telling me so much about the Soane family.

One of the churchwardens of St Martin's, Kentish Town, who has witnessed several vestry brawls without presenting anyone to the Archdeacon for participating, will be relieved that this book is finished and he no longer has to listen to endless tales from his wife about the long dead.

I am grateful to Patric Dickinson, the *Richmond Herald*, who encouraged me to write down my probate tales and has watched the progress of the book with interest.

I would like to thank the Vicar of St Martin's, Kentish Town, who performed my father's funeral rites with such a gentle certainty, when I was trying to finish this book, that I was able to do so. And unlike his seventeenth-century counterpart (see chapter 4), he certainly did not 'reel and stagger at the grave'.

Finally, comes almost every family historian I have ever met. The study of history can be, and often is, a dryasdust affair. When seen through the eyes of those whose fascination with the past is a personal matter, it changes and takes on life. It would be nice to think that there are descendants living from Ann Hooper who charged half a crown a go in Wapping Wall, from Betty Bourke who ran off with a handsome soldier, or even from Dirty Doll Winterbottom of Shoreditch.

A Note on the Use of Source Material

The stories in this book are taken from the evidence of witnesses in lawsuits, many of them uneducated and as many probably bribed or threatened by the litigants. In the case of the slander actions particularly, there is a great deal of repetition and confusion in the different depositions. I have highlighted what was supposedly said by the parties and endeavoured to make sense of the varying and conflicting accounts. Where I have taken sides, and I almost always agree with the Civilians, it will be evident from the text.

The only liberties I have taken with truth are as follows: I am not sure that Mistress Anderson showed her injuries to Elizabeth Bentley (see chapter 3), but it sounds as if she did. I am not certain that St John's Street was slippery in October 1698 (see chapter 4), but I do know that it was snowing and foggy.

I have retained the original spelling but inserted punctuation, to help make sense of it all.

Sources for material in the text of this book, including references for documents in the Public Record Office, are listed in the bibliography. Sources for illustrations are shown in the relevant captions.

'Vy don't you pitch into her, Sarah?' A not very neighbourly altercation at Seven Dials; described by Dickens in *Sketches by Boz* (1836-1837), and illustrated here by George Cruikshank

Introduction

A Dickensian world

THE STORIES to be told in the following pages come from the records of some London law courts. Charles Dickens worked as a clerk in those courts and was familiar with the 'sundry immense books of evidence' produced there.

In the spring of 1829 he took up employment with a lawyer called Charles Fenton in the institution known as Doctors' Commons. Later he set himself up as a freelance shorthand writer, transcribing proceedings in court for clients.

Doctors' Commons was the name given to the buildings near St Paul's Cathedral which housed the College of Advocates, the courts, registries and chambers of the practitioners of the Civil Law, a breed now extinct. There wills were proved or disputed and family squabbles and feuds orchestrated. For fat fees the advocates and proctors, the equivalent of barristers and solicitors, would untie impossible marriages and see that reluctant grooms were held to casual engagement promises. Punishments were administered for sexual irregularities and for calling one's neighbour rude names. By an accident of history, the same select bunch of prestigious lawyers who, under the aegis of the Church, pried into the most intimate and painful corners of family life, also presided over matters which came before the High Court of Admiralty.

Dickens's biographers have rather neglected this aspect of his life and the impact it made on him. They say that he is silent about the period of his career when he was working first in the Church courts and then in the House of Commons. Certainly he does not have much to say in his books about Parliament, but there is plenty to be found in his writings which comes directly from his experience in and around Doctors' Commons.

No one seems to be quite sure how long he was there; the *Law List* keeps him at 5 Bell Yard up to 1844, but the general opinion is that he was only there for a few years. However long it was, he later spoke of this period as the 'usefullest of my life'. All human life paraded in that 'lazy nook near St Paul's' for the young man's delectation. The characters and stories he encountered in court and in the records slipped into his imagination. *Sketches by Boz* contains a straightforward journalist's description of the place, and in *Our Mutual Friend*, *David Copperfield* and *Pickwick Papers* recollections from the Commons are pulled out and fashioned as fiction.

There is a postscript to *Our Mutual Friend*:

There is sometimes an odd disposition in this country to dispute as improbable in fiction, what are the commonest experiences in fact. Therefore, I note here . . . that there are hundreds of will cases (as they are called), far more remarkable than that fancied in this Book.

Just a few of those remarkable tales are told in *this* book.

As Dickens's journalist, Boz, walked home from Doctors' Commons he fell into a train of reflection 'Upon the curious old records of likings and dislikings; of jealousies and revenges; of affection defying the power of death, and hatred pursued beyond the grave.'

The young Charles Dickens at about the time of his first employment at Doctors' Commons.
Miniature by Janet Barrow (1830).
(Reproduced by courtesy of the Dickens House Museum, London)

A Windy Day by Robert Dighton. Scene outside Bowles's print shop, St Paul's Churchyard, one of the draughtiest spots in London. (Courtesy of the Board of Trustees of the V&A)

1

Setting the Scene

'A fossil state'

IN CHARLES DICKENS'S DAY, when Londoners spoke of 'the Commons' they were not usually referring to Parliament, but to an awesome and secluded agglomeration of legal buildings which lay between St Paul's Cathedral and the Thames. There, until 1867, the courts of Civil Law heard probate, matrimonial, slander and sexual and clerical disciplinary actions. The registries of various church officials issued marriage licences and probates and the High Court of Admiralty dealt with maritime causes.

Doctors' Commons is the background for the events described in this book, the place where the miseries and private concerns of our ancestors had a public airing; perhaps the site is haunted still by anguished ghosts.

If you stand by the statue of Queen Anne at the west front of St Paul's and face south towards the Thames, opposite you, on the other side of the road, is Dean's Court. That corner, according to an old tale, was a draughty spot; the Devil, long ago, rode here on the wind, dismounted, and left his blustery steed waiting for him. He found the company at Doctors' Commons so congenial that he stayed while the wind howled impatiently for his return.

The main entrance to Doctors' Commons was not through Dean's Court, but along the remnant of an ancient lane which led down to the river bank. These days it is called Godliman Street, but it was known as Paul's Chain in years gone by, because a chain used to be put across the road at the time of divine service in the cathedral to keep out the noisy carts and wagons which rumbled along the lane that crossed it. Along the west side of Godliman Street stands a monster building which houses British Telecom. On the other side of the road a brazen neighbour announces itself as the Nikko Bank plc. Through the middle of these two buildings runs the remains of Knightrider Street, where once, according to the topographer, John Stow, knights rode on their way from the Tower Royal to tournaments in Smithfield. In later centuries this was the heart of Doctors' Commons.

The wind no longer whistles round Dean's Court. It has not whistled for well over a hundred years, as you will learn from the blue plaque on the south side of the British Telecom building in Queen Victoria Street. 'This', it says, 'is the site of Doctors' Commons, demolished 1867.' Presumably those who erected the plaque thought no words of explanation were required. There is no modern equivalent to the Commons, and it is fortunate that so distinguished a guide as Dickens is available. Let us go back to the 1830s, when the young legal clerk first took up his post.

The Last of Doctors' Commons, as illustrated in the *Daily Graphic* of 3 October 1894. St Paul's Cathedral is glimpsed above the partly demolished walls. (Greater London Record Office)

Doctors' Commons in 1830

It is a wintry afternoon in the cathedral precinct, enclosed by high walls and thronged with busy people: men in tall hats and greatcoats, errand boys, ladies in bonnets and shawls. The sound is the clatter of hooves on the cobbles, the creak of hackney carriages and the cries of street hawkers. Yellow fog is rolling up from the river and you can hear the hooting of ships in the distance. Across Paul's Chain there is a little low arch, with a French hotel on one corner and a bookshop on the other. The arch is guarded by two men in long white aprons. One appears to be accosting an elderly, portly gentleman wearing a broad-brimmed hat, a green shawl and a nosegay in his buttonhole. He is trying to sell a marriage licence to Tony Weller (from *Pickwick Papers*):

Where the Devil tied up his blustery steed: the entrance to Doctors' Commons. (The Guildhall Library, London)

'Licence, sir? Licence, sir?'

'What licence?'

'Marriage licence, I think you want one, sir.'

'Dash my veskit, I never thought o' that.'

After a few minutes' conversation they go off together, under the arch (which incidentally, sports a written warning against marriage touts) and down the hill, away from the bustle into a series of paved stone courts lined with fine old red-brick houses, some dating from the time of the 'merry monarch'. Let us follow them into that dignified world of privilege and neat gardens. Lean, harassed clerks scuttle about with fat, untidy bundles of papers tied up with pink tape. Here and there a wig and a gown may swing by in superior conversation with another such. The fog is bringing the darkness early and the lamp-lighter is doing his rounds; you can still just about make out what is written on the brass plates on the doors as you pass by.

At 3 Paul's Chain is the Registry of the Archdeacon of Surrey, open from 10 in the morning to 4 in the afternoon. As the street slopes down to the river we pass the offices and registries of many ecclesiastical officials, the Bishops of London and Winchester, the Archdeacons of London, Middlesex and Rochester, the Deans and Chapters of Westminster and St Paul's, and many others.

At 6 Great Knightrider Street is a modest house in the classical style, but large enough to accommodate a staff of some seventy souls and a busy public search room. This is the Prerogative Office, the senior probate registry; it closes at 3 pm in winter as the main public business is the searching of wills, for which a good light is necessary and candles too much of a fire risk. Records here go back to Chaucer's day. A narrow passage leads through the house, out into a small garden and then into the main building which contains a strong room and a public search room. This room is long and well lit by windows overlooking the gardens. It is partitioned off, on either side, into a series of boxes used by copying clerks and, down the middle of the room, is a row of high desks where the public, mainly lawyers' clerks, consult the vellum-bound will indexes. Thirty thousand searches were made in 1829.

Little work has been done here today. As no artificial light is allowed, a foggy day is an idle day, a day for gossip. The clerks, who do piece-work and usually do not have a minute to spare, will have been wandering about with their hands in their pockets chatting and exchanging titbits of news.

A red-brick arch marks the entry to College Square, which is dominated by the Common Hall with its court room, library and refectory. Most of the courts sit in session here now; the Prerogative Court, which is the busiest by far, every day. In times past they all had their formal hearings in churches or cathedrals, the Bishop of London's courts sat in the 'consistorial place' in St Paul's, for instance; the Archdeacon of London presided at Christchurch by Newgate; and the appeal Court of Arches sat in St Mary le Bow, with the doctors arrayed in velvet and ermine. The ecclesiastical registries have been in Doctors' Commons longer than the courts.

Today's hearings are over, so we can go into the court room; it resembles a chapel, with dark, polished wainscoting stretching high up the walls. Above it hang the coats of arms of the Doctors of Civil Law, gilded and glimmering in the faint shafts of light which filter through from the lamps outside. The room is divided into two by wooden arches forming a sort of rood screen; behind the screen is a horseshoe-shaped platform. Had we been here a little earlier we might have seen, as Boz did, an array of old gentlemen with red gowns and wigs sitting on old-fashioned dining chairs round this platform, a winking owl of a judge in the middle. Below the doctors sit the proctors in black, with wigs and white cravats, like a flock of magpies. The stove is still chirping in the centre of the room; it seems a quiet, sleepy, cosy place.

To learn what went on in the court room and behind those mysterious brass plates, we will turn first to the pages of *David Copperfield*, the most autobiographical of Dickens's novels.

David, like Dickens, went to work in the office of a firm of proctors. In those days, before the young Victoria had ascended the throne, and not very long after Napoleon had been trounced, Doctors' Commons was a well known institution. That is not to say that the man in the street had much idea

The Common Hall at Doctors' Commons, by Thomas Rowlandson and Auguste Pugin, 1808. (The Guildhall Library, London)

of what went on in the complex to the south of St Paul's churchyard, except perhaps that it was something to do with marriages and wills, and David was no exception. Even after he had made up his mind to enter a career there, he was not really clear as to what that career would be or, indeed, what a proctor was. His worldly-wise school chum, Steerforth, explained:

> A proctor is a gentlemanly sort of fellow . . . he is a sort of monkish attorney. He is to some faded courts held in Doctors' Commons . . . what solicitors are to the courts of law and equity. He is a functionary whose existence, in the natural course of things, would have terminated about two hundred years ago.

The proctors were indeed very gentlemanly and wealthy; the ermine which trimmed their black court dress marked them out as superior by far to their humble brothers, the ordinary solicitors. They were a most select elite: in 1832 there were only just over one hundred of them in the profession, whereas there were thousands of ordinary attorneys. It is a matter of considerable doubt as to whether or not the profession was redundant by the time of Charles I, but Steerforth was no historian.

Those faded courts, he continued, are in a 'little out-of-the way place, where they administer what is called ecclesiastical law'. He was not quite right; although all the courts in the Commons were Church courts, except, of course the High Court of Admiralty, the law administered there, as was explained to a Chancery Commission a decade or so after Dickens wrote *David Copperfield*, was an amalgam of Civil Law (a descendant of Roman law which was practised on the Continent), church or canon law and precedent. One of the lawyers who gave evidence to the Commission implied that the eminent doctors made it up as they went along; 'There are no books', he said 'from which the practice might be learnt'.

Steerforth explained further:

> There . . . they . . . play all kinds of tricks with obsolete old monsters of Acts of Parliament, which three fourths of the world know nothing about, and the other fourth suppose to have been dug up in a fossil state in the days of the Edwards. It's a place that has an ancient monopoly in suits about people's wills and people's marriages, and disputes about ships and boats.

He goes on:

> You shall go down there one day and find them blundering through half the nautical terms in Young's Dictionary, apropos of the Nancy having run down the Sarah Jane . . . and you shall go there another day, and find them deep in the evidence pro and con, respecting a clergyman who has misbehaved himself, and you shall find the judge in the nautical case, the advocate in the clergyman's case, or contrarywise. They are like actors: now a man's a judge; now he's one thing, now he's another; now he's something else, change and change about, but it's always a very pleasant profitable affair of private theatricals.

If we examine the brass plates in Knightrider Street and its environs and the names in the *Law List*, we will find that Steerforth was right. Fifteen courts had their registries in the Commons and most of them sat in the Common Hall by 1830. They were serviced by about a hundred proctors and thirty advocates, many of whom came from old Commons families. It was quite usual for the judge in one court to plead in another. By the nineteenth century it was very much the preserve of a few families, a close corporation united by ties of affinity.

Sir Herbert Jenner Fust, who reminded Dickens of a blinking owl, and whose girth and red face he ascribed to good living, was the most senior Civilian of his day, Dean of the Arches and Judge of the Prerogative. His income was commensurate with his elevated position, £3,500 per year, £1,000 more than the salaries of the joint secretaries to the Treasury. More than a few members of Sir Herbert's family had their practice in the Commons, and in fact, *The Times* remarked that the whole place might be aptly renamed the 'Court of the Jenners'.

The four Moore brothers, relatives of John Moore, who had been Archbishop of Canterbury before Dickens was born, held, jointly, the office of Registrar of the Prerogative, in return for emoluments of £8,000 a year, although the post had long ceased to be anything but a sinecure.

Fees were high; customers were paying for a skilled professional service and, as Steerforth pointed out, it was a monopoly business. If an estate came under the jurisdiction of one of the courts in the Commons, there was no way a will could be proved except through the offices of a firm of proctors. The proving and registering of a straightforward will was, Dickens tells us, a 'very light and lucrative business'. For probate of a short will in 1817, on an estate valued under £5, you would have to pay 8s. 6d, if you came in person to the registry, and 17s. if you wanted to take the necessary oath by commission near home. (It would be misleading to translate these charges into modern terms with any degree of certainty. A very rough idea of the extent of the PCC's fees can be achieved working solely on the basis of a labourer's wage, now and then. In 1817 a labourer earned about 11s. a week, now perhaps £200. If we take a £5 estate as being worth £1,820 in modern terms, then the 17s. payable for probate by commission becomes £309. 6s., or 16 per cent.)

There was a sliding scale, but the relative cost of proving a will of £10,000 was much less than was paid on a small estate. If the document was longer than four sheets an extra 2s. a sheet was charged, and if it had not been attested by two witnesses an extra 25s. had to be paid. Grants of administration made if no will was left, were more expensive than probate.

As far as litigation was concerned, if you wanted some matrimonial, probate or nautical business done, in most cases you were bound to go to the Commons and use the services of one of the thirty advocates licensed to plead. At common law and equity there were many more barristers to choose from.

Procedure in suits was protracted. Dickens used a case which he had transcribed himself in the London Commissary Court as the basis for the story of the little ginger-beer seller involved in a vestry brawl that he recounts in *Sketches by Boz*. The production of no less than twenty-eight affidavits resulted in the victim being sentenced to the 'awful punishment' of a fortnight's excommunication.

Dickens portrays a corrupt and obsolete organisation; *Punch* compared it to a knacker's yard and spoke of the proctors as 'necessary evils' so long as the testamentary law stays in its 'present abominable state'. Soon after, the arrogant, complacent Commons were swept away; a Principal Probate Registry was set up under state auspices in 1858 and the rest of the business was transferred to the Court of Chancery. It was time for reform, but Dickens's vivid images of 'conceit and silliness', and rich, idle, stupid lawyers, should be tempered. To set the scene properly for the stories in this book, it is necessary to explain something of the history and nature of the goings on which seemed so ludicrous and wicked to the young shorthand writer and to many of his contemporaries.

The history of the courts

Although the Reformation saw the handing over of many medieval ecclesiastical activities to other bodies, the Church still continued to exercise social control and to interfere in aspects of everyday life. Attendance at church, for instance, was not just an occasion for devotion, but an obligation under the law, a way of regularly 'signing on' as a member of the parish. Shakespeare's father was, like thousands of others, prosecuted for not going to church; in his case it was for 'fear of process for debt'. Public announcements such as royal proclamations were read from the pulpit or pinned up in the porch. It was in church or through the bishop that intentions to marry were registered, to avoid bigamy and other irregularities which might be the occasion of fatherless children being 'thrown on the parish'. Likewise, fornicators and adulterers were made to perform a shaming public penance in church.

Churchwardens were important local officials who came knocking on your door to collect local taxes and might report you to a higher authority if you misbehaved. The Church, through the parish organisation, provided social security, police, a 'citizens' advice bureau', counselling, and much more besides. Over and above that was a network of Church courts dealing with probate, morals and matters of clerical discipline with Doctors' Commons at its head.

Between three and four hundred courts administered church law in England and Wales. They were of various sorts and sizes with a complicated network of relationships to one another. Some parish clergy held their own courts, usually by virtue of being the 'heir' of some abbey which had ruled over the morals and last wishes of the local inhabitants. In some places the right to prove wills lay with the lord of the manor, whose antecedents had perhaps bought monastic land or rights at the time of the Dissolution. All archdeacons and bishops had courts, as did the deans and chapters of cathedrals. At the top of the pyramid were the provincial courts of Canterbury and York, with the Arches and the high Court of Delegates for appeal.

There was a wide range of suits, both party against party actions and those brought by the court itself against individuals. The latter, ex officio actions, as they were known, though quite common from the Middle Ages to the early seventeenth century, virtually disappeared after the Restoration. Not all of the courts were empowered to act in all the types of actions available. Matrimonial cases, legal separation, breach of promise, etc., had to go to the bishop's court or higher. Some courts had no probate jurisdiction and others had only that.

This is not the place for a learned exposition on the nature of business conducted in church vestries and the 'consistorial places'. Suffice it to say that, at some time or other, the following came under the purview of God's justices: refusal to pay church rates, tithe suits, dereliction of duty by churchwardens or parish clerks, unseemly behaviour in church, working or rowdy drinking on Sunday, neglecting to have children baptised, adultery, fornica-

The Consistory Court, Chester Cathedral. (Pitkin Pictorials (photograph: Sydney W Newbery))

tion, incest, simony, heresy, witchcraft, bearing a bastard, all matrimonial suits, some sorts of slander, usury, the disposal of the personal estate of the dead (probate), all matters concerning the fabric and interior of churches, all matters of clergy discipline.

In times past brushes with the church courts were as common as parking fines are today; Shakespeare's family was well acquainted with the 'bawdy court' at Stratford-upon-Avon. The 'consistorial place' in Chester Cathedral is a fine court room. The steps up to it have been worn right down by the many thousands who went before the bishop or his lawyers, sitting in grim solemnity. At the other end of the scale is the apse of the tiny church of Witham Friary in Somerset. There the incumbent, who had inherited the probate jurisdiction of the local Carthusian monastery, sat to check through the wills left by the farmers in the village.

Dickens was far from the first to find fault with the church courts; they always had a bad press, as any organisation which interferes with private fun and family money is bound to have. From the Middle Ages to the seventeenth century, it was the messengers of the courts who, as the bearers of bad tidings, bore the brunt of popular dislike. The summoner, or apparitor as he was later known, was the official who came to the door and handed over the fearful sealed parchment document, written in the magically powerful language that the Church and its officials used.

Witham Friary church, Somerset, by Philip Croker, from *Monastic Remains* (1824) by Sir Richard Colt Hoare

The English note attached to the Latin document might tell you that you must go up to the Prerogative Court in London to explain why you had not paid your cousin the £2 your father had left him. It might be an order to go before the archdeacon to answer the rumours spread by the folk in the village about you and the baker's daughter last haymaking. If your wife had lost her temper with the woman next door and accused her of entertaining men at 'unseasonable hours', then the note might be a summons for both of you to appear to defend a defamation action.

Chaucer's summoner (the official who issued summonses to the church court), one of the pilgrims in *The Canterbury Tales* (*c*. 1387), was a lecherous, narrow-eyed, garlic-munching monster, whose acne was so bad that children were frightened of him. When he was in drink, which he often was, he would speak nothing but Latin, repeating by rote the few words he had picked up in court and from the citations he had to deliver. As Chaucer said of him:

> And eek ye knowen wel how that a jay
> Kan clepen 'Watte' as wel as kan the pope.
> ('A jay can say "what" as well as the Pope can'.)

But, added the poet ironically, he was a good chap. In exchange for only a quart of wine, he would let anyone keep a mistress for a whole year and, for a small financial consideration, all fears of excommunication would be put at rest.

Chaucer was writing at a time when Church officials were being attacked for corrupt practices and laxity. A hundred years later, when religious reforms were underway, the officers of the Church took on a more sinister role. The apparitor's knock might be the beginning of a nightmare which ended up with a human bonfire in Smithfield. In Bloody Mary's day, even casual conversation could be dangerous. Two women were examined before the London Consistory and referred to Star Chamber for saying they had heard a new baby utter the words 'fast and pray'. They agreed to recant and had to go before a crowd in St Paul's Churchyard and confirm that the child had not really spoken, but had merely 'groaned and rattled in the throat . . . and died'.

The bad old days of the Marian burnings and the years of threatened Spanish invasion which followed, made seventeenth-century Englishmen deeply mistrustful of 'popery' and nervous of bishops, ceremonial and anything which smacked of church power overreaching itself. Archbishop Laud's High Church reforms and extensive use of the courts to enforce them exacerbated the situation, and the church courts were abolished during the Interregnum. Not that Doctors' Commons stood idle. The lawyers there were awarded the prize of all the probate business from the whole country. The folk of Witham Friary would now have to send their wills up to London instead of just handing them over to the vicar.

The Church of England with all its legal paraphernalia came back with the Restoration in 1660 and the courts were as unpopular as ever. At the time of the 'Popish Plot' (1678) a pamphleteer claimed that it was St Augustine, 'Austin the Monk', who had started the Church's meddling with coercive power. Ever since he cursed the monks of Bangor with bell, book and candle, churchmen have used their courts to murder and destroy for religion's sake. The courts are expensive and illegal:

> What colour have the Bishops in their Spiritual Courts . . . to send out Process under their own seals as if they were paramount the King, and even as big as the Pope himself? So runs their Process viz. I cite you to appear before me etc. at such a place. Now I would feign know what this I is, where it be I Pope, or I Jesuit, or I Turk.

The pamphleteer concludes his polemic: 'I have never heard of any Good ever did come from those Courts, but many have been ruined and undone by them.' Doctor Johnson, writing a hundred years later, was in agreement. When he read his tragedy of Irene to the Registrar of the Lichfield court, the latter asked of the heroine: 'How can you possibly contrive to plunge her into deeper calamity?' 'Sir', replied Johnson, 'I can put her into the Spiritual Court!'

Complaints about exorbitant fees were regularly levelled at the Civilians. Charges could be high, as we have seen, especially in the nineteenth century, but lawyers are always accused of lining their pockets. The authorities made repeated attempts to keep probate costs at a reasonable, standard rate. A sliding scale of charges had been introduced by Archbishop Chichele in the fourteenth century and this was reviewed from time to time. Grants on estates classified as poor could be bought for a minimal cost. David Copperfield's father-in-law, Spenlow the proctor, with his lucrative probate business, had a mansion in Norwood with champagne on tap and dark brown East India sherry, precious enough to make a man wink. On the other hand, the Surrey Consistory gave John Ruskin's wife an annulment for only £2 12s.

Much of the cost incurred by the clients in litigation was occasioned by the custom of examining numbers of witnesses. Dickens thought it was ridiculous: twenty-eight affidavits were taken in his fictional vestry brawl case. When Spenlow showed David Copperfield round the Commons, the London Consistory was sifting evidence twice the length of *Robinson Crusoe*. The proctor confided that the most profitable business was a good case of a disputed will, with a 'neat little estate of thirty of forty thousand pounds'. Not only did such a case supply pretty pickings in the way of arguments at every stage of proceedings, with mountain upon mountain of evidence, but it was likely to be pursued in a lively and spirited manner as all costs would be born by the estate.

There were many who defended the rules of proof and the method of taking written evidence in the Civilian courts as being scrupulous and thorough. There had to be two witnesses at least to every fact and the evidence of the principal parties, while not discounted, was held to be unreliable. Deponents had to provide a good deal of autobiographical information so that the value of their evidence might be properly assessed. A general statement, or examination 'in chief', was taken from them, privately in chambers, and then they had to answer a list of numbered questions. All evidence was written down before the court hearing and copies of it circulated to the lawyers involved.

It was the opinion of the Civilian, Doctor Brown, that the church courts' procedure was more likely to get at the truth than *nisi prius* cases where there was live cross-examination and 'Every incautious or hasty impression is instantly bellowed to the jury'.

Arguably the justice dispensed in the Commons, though expensive, was the finest in the land, serviced as it was by a highly skilled bar and bench. According to the 1854 Chancery Commission 'anything at all difficult' in matters of probate was, by now, referred to the Prerogative Court and the London Consistory Court had, by the second half of the seventeenth century, become the 'divorce court' for the whole country. The letter of the law was flexible and the proceedings allowed for a rigorous investigation of the facts. However small the case the same thoroughness applied, whether it was a sailor's widow trying to get the few pounds owed her by the Navy, a fight over a millionaire's fortune, or a coachman's wife defending her good name.

Over the centuries, many of those matters which the church courts had supervised with such care were appropriated by other bodies or ceased to be of public concern. The type of church 'policing' which peaked in the sixteenth and seventeenth centuries came to an end. Long forgotten is the smell of faggots from Smithfield. No one has been paraded before his or her neighbours wearing the white sheet of penance for two hundred years or more. Slander and tithe were gradually taken over by the king's court, and probate and marriage were taken over by the state in the mid-nineteenth century. Doctors' Commons was razed to the ground as if it had never been.

Church courts still meet; you may catch the Arches in the crypt of St Mary le Bow, a small, informal group of elderly men in suits, no ermine or scarlet. The *Guardian* reported on 29 November 1990 that an unrepentant vicar had been sacked for adultery by the 'rarely convened' Consistory meeting at Chichester.

The piles of depositions and other paperwork which accumulated over the years are a monument to an extinct legal system. More than that, they document the everyday lives and concerns of all sorts and conditions of people, not, as one might imagine, just men of wealth and status.

Billingsgate fishwives living up to their reputation. 'Language' from George Cruikshank's *Phrenological Illustrations* (1826)

The courts of wives, widows and servants

Wandering around the alleys and courtyards of Knightrider Street in the heyday of Doctors' Commons, it is remarkable how many women one encounters. Some are dressed in silks and velvets, borne in sedan chairs or carriages. Others have walked over from Wapping or Clerkenwell, or come on the mail coach from the outlying villages of Hendon or Hampstead; they wear dull, workaday clothes.

These are no ordinary law courts where men of business and property conduct their affairs. In the probate courts and registries, the preponderance of custom is female. Men are the property owners; they die and, in the overwhelming majority of cases, their wives are appointed executrixes. If disputes arise, it is those widows who often become involved in the litigation. By the seventeenth century, in cases of intestacy the wife is almost invariably preferred to any male relative as the administratrix of her husband's goods. When a wife or widow dies, more often than not, no recourse is had to law. She often has little to leave, the disposition of property having already been dealt with by her husband, giving her a life interest only.

'Evidence of the most intimate nature'. A parlour maid, *c.*1743, serves tea and eavesdrops. Engraving by Trunchy, after F Hayman. (Reproduced in *Social Caricatures in the Eighteenth Century* (1905) by George Paston)

As far as slander actions are concerned, those conducted here are almost entirely brought by women and usually against women, often ordinary working women, coachmen's wives, washerwomen, hairdressers, silk throwsters and barmaids.

In the 'divorce court', the Consistory Court, one would expect the genders to be equally balanced, but even here, before the mid-eighteenth century, there are more women around. Wives, before then, were more commonly the initiating party and many suits were quickly dropped and settled out of court before the offending husband was required to appear.

Many of the young, rough-clad lasses are here as witnesses. Probate and marriage litigation requires evidence of the most intimate nature. It is the household servants, especially personal maids and girls involved in the presentation of meals, who are most likely to have been there when master hit mistress with a candlestick, or mistress entertained the dancing master in her bedchamber. Probate litigation is often just as much a trial of love as any matrimonial suit. As the widow fights her brother-in-law for her deceased husband's nest-egg, who but the chamber-maid can give the firmest evidence of the signs of affection exchanged between the couple? The person most likely to have been in the room when the dying man uttered those words which left all to his niece by marriage was, of course, the nurse-keeper who attended him in his last illness.

'Petticoat evidence'. From *The Genteel Habits of England* (*c*.1640), by Edmund Marmion.
(The Master and Fellows, Magdalene College, Cambridge)

Doctors' Commons then, could have been nicknamed the 'court of wives, widows and servants'. If we dip into the piles of petticoat evidence we should surely be able to get a true flavour of the female experience.

In theory a woman's property passed to her husband at marriage; her children were his to dispose of, her body was his to use and abuse. She could be beaten (reasonably), locked up and abandoned if she took a lover for solace. And there was no escape.

However horrific the legal manuals might seem to modern woman, our ancestresses were never quite the slaves that the letter of the law painted them. 'The law supposes', says Oliver's grandfather in *Oliver Twist*, 'that a wife acts under the direction of her husband'. Mr Bumble makes his famous reply that, in that case 'the law is a ass'.

There were always ways that caring fathers and mothers could tie their sons-in-law up in legal knots, which kept their daughter's property under her control. Private separation deeds and other records indicate that mothers, particularly of young children, often had custody if not legal control of the children. The law made sure that deserted wives and widows were well maintained; alimony was normally set at one-third of the husband's income, the same proportion which was assigned as dower and the same share as the widow got of her husband's personal estate if he died intestate. If there were

The marriage settlement, though not perhaps as Millamant would have drafted it. From *Marriage à la Mode* (1745), by William Hogarth

no children she got two-thirds and was invariably allowed to live in the matrimonial home until she died. For the gentry the strict settlement, which established itself during the seventeenth century, guaranteed an annual revenue for the wife, based on her jointure. For all classes there were ways for a woman to escape from an intolerable union.

Perhaps more significant than any of this is the undoubted existence of many a strong-minded, intelligent and forceful woman. Millamant, in William Congreve's *The Way of the World*, expresses some very clear ideas as to what should be written into a marriage contract, a reminder, perhaps, that Congreve had an affair with Sarah, Duchess of Marlborough, one of the most powerful forces in the land.

They are but trifles, she insists:

> Liberty to pay and receive letters, without interrogatories or wry
> faces on your part; to wear what I please; and chuse conversation
> with regard only to my own taste; to have no obligations upon me
> to converse with wits that I don't like, because they are your
> acquaintances; or to be intimate with fools because they may be
> your relations. To come to dinner when I please, dine in my
> dressing room when I am out of humour, without giving a reason.
> To have my closet inviolate; to be sole empress of my tea table
> which you must never presume to approach without first asking
> leave. And lastly, wherever I am, you shall always knock at the door
> before you come in.

These articles subscribed, she admits the possibility of 'dwindling into a wife'.

The records of the Commons abound with independent women, many of them working wives, who were common among the artisan classes. In the Restoration period, for instance sailors' and textile workers' wives from the East End almost all seem to have worked to supplement their husbands' incomes, running vegetable stalls and alehouses, working as hairdressers, nurses and cleaners.

Mary Sydenham (who was married to a tailor, but ran her own laundry business for the lawyers of the Temple, and had done well enough to be able to rent a substantial house for £14 a year) gave evidence to the Prerogative Court in 1666 for a friend and neighbour who was trying to get hold of the £1,000 her dead husband had left.

The dead man, one Thomas Grey, had been a surgeon and, like many of his profession, made a fortune by treating victims of the Great Plague, and then succumbing to the disease himself. According to Mary he was both a drinker and a gambler, neither of which is to be wondered at when one considers the perilous nature of his occupation. One day, Mary told the court: 'the said Thomas Grey, coming home in drink, did demand moneys of his wife, whom he usually intrusted with the keeping of it.' She 'refusing then to give him any, supposing he would lose it at gaming, to which he was addicted, hee, the said deceased, did fall out with Elizabeth, his wife, and seemed to be very angry with her'. The mistress clearly held the purse-strings in that household.

The domestic authority of the powerful wife was something which, then as now, intimidated the misogynist. In the 1660s, when Poplar was the East India Company's 'stockbroker belt', an old bachelor called John Meeks, an Oxford MA, lived in a house in North Street. He had little time for his family, who were inclined to jeer at him, and took up with a young tanner called Jonathan Magwicke, with whom he planned to set up home. On Meeks's death Magwicke made a play for the bachelor's estate and litigation ensued at the Commons. A local farrier, one of the many witnesses, repeated a revealing exchange he had held with the bachelor Meeks:

FARRIER: I wonder Jonathan Magwicke does not marry. He will undoe himself to do as he does, to keep a house and a maid and men and no guide.

MEEKS: Marry? What should he marry for? If he will be ruled by me I will make him the best Tanner on this side of the country.

Single women often seem to have led their own lives without necessarily having recourse to male relatives for protection, shelter or financial support. A fairly typical case in the Prerogative Court, a few years after the Restoration, was that which concerned the estate of Martha Lancashire.

Martha was unmarried and of independent means. When she became ill, she went to lodge with her cousin, Margaret Brandred, in her house in St Stephen Coleman. She had no other relatives except a sister, Dorothy, who was 'affected with melancholy and at several times by Intervall distempered in her mind therewith'. On her death-bed Martha revealed that she had several hundred pounds to bequeath, and she wanted most of it to go to her cousin, Margaret, with only a small legacy for her sister. The melancholy Dorothy contested the nuncupative (spoken) will and there was sinister talk of sharp spasms in the deceased's stomach just before she died, only half an hour after the will was made. Evidence was given by two women, one a middle-aged Lancashire wife, who lived in Old Jewry and had met Margaret Brandred when she was working in the shop where the latter was apprenticed. The other was the widow who lodged with Margaret.

There is nothing particularly 'liberated' about all this, but it is perhaps worth noting that there are no men involved, except, of course, the lawyers.

No doubt there were many, like Sarah Lambeth, a Southampton sailor's wife, giving evidence in a probate case, who found it convenient to be a *feme covert*. She was a resourceful woman who earned her own living by buying and selling a variety of commodities during her husband's long absences. When the examiner asked how much she was worth, reluctant to answer, as witness- es tended to be, she had the perfect excuse: 'She doth not know herself to be worth anything because all that she hath in her power doth of right belong to her husband.'

It could be useful to be a *feme covert*, and most women were, but it could be hell on earth. For a taste of what some individuals suffered behind closed doors we will go into the Consistory Court and meet some husbands and wives.

A cynical alliance. From *A Rake's Progress* (1735), by William Hogarth

2
At the Court of Marriage
Husbands and wives at the Consistory

THERE WAS RELIEF from unendurable suffering in marriage, for various escape routes were open to the desperate and the determined. You could run away and set up home with someone else and, in a society where secret marriage and bigamy were rife, if the churchwarden was not alerted, you could probably marry again without anyone being the wiser. Marriage was a fluid affair until Lord Hardwicke's act of 1753 brought it firmly under control of Church and State. Contract marriage, a simple private agreement between a couple, could be defended in law, and for couples who agreed to differ, the local attorney would draw a private deed of separation.

For those who did not agree, the Civilians offered a legal separation, a divorce from bed and board. There could be no remarriage, but the parties could live apart and alimony was awarded to the 'divorced' woman who was, thereafter, treated at law as a *feme sole*.

It was with the making and unmaking of marriages that Doctors' Commons was chiefly associated in the public mind from the late seventeenth century. Marriage licences were issued from the Vicar General's office there and the London Consistory Court assumed a virtual monopoly in matrimonial suits.

For these stories from the Commons we will look at some 'jealousies and revenges' between husbands and wives, becoming historical voyeurs, peeping through keyholes and cracks. We will press our ears up against the wall to catch the whispers exchanged by servant girls as they sit by the kitchen fire listening to the muffled screams from the bedchamber above.

Domestic violence in seventeenth-century London

Samuel Pepys and his wife had a turbulent relationship and there is reference in his diary to papers which were drawn when they briefly separated. A distant cousin of Samuel Pepys, Charles Pepys, fared far worse and was taken to the Commons by his unhappy wife.

It is the summer of 1686, an uneasy time for London with the old king's popish brother, James II, on the throne. For the Pepys household, living over their tobacconist shop in a yard off Lombard Street, there were horrors and distress enough at home to keep their minds off worries about Jesuits in the sewers. Charles and Mary Pepys had been married for seven years and several children had been born; Charles had a teenage daughter from a previous liaison or marriage. Mary was twenty-six and came from a well-to-do family; her mother lived close by. Another baby had arrived in March, but had only survived five weeks. The Pepys family were in debt as their previous shop had been burned down about eighteen months previously and Charles had had to rebuild it, replace his stock and finance the repairs which had to be done to his neighbours' houses.

What City gentleman pushing open the door of that shop with its jingling bell, sniffing the good smell of tobacco and viewing with satisfaction the rows of gleaming jars and racks of clay pipes would have guessed at the goings-on in that respectable establishment?

When Mary could no longer endure the punishments inflicted on her by her brutal husband she went to a lawyer in the Commons, one Crespy, and proceedings were initiated. Servants and friends were called in to bear witness, about eleven for Mary, ten of them women, and eight for Charles, all men and one barmaid. These are the tales they told: first the women's story.

A baby was born to Mary in March 1686. His head and neck, said Ann Boomer, who nursed the Pepys children, were all black because of the violent treatment the mother had been subjected to during her pregnancy. While she was lying in Charles would go and see her and 'fall a cursing and swearing at her' and 'put her into a passion of crying, that they knew not what to do with her'. The baby did not live for very long.

One summer morning, not long after the baby's death, the family's nineteen-year-old servant, Dorothy, was busy in the kitchen when she heard her mistress shriek 'Murder'. She ran upstairs and there was Mr Pepys, who had been out drinking all night, with his wife held down across two chairs. Her head clothes were pulled off and he was battering her bare head against the window. She was choking on the blood which was pouring out of her mouth. The girl tried to intervene; the master lurched across and hit her and told her he would break her neck if she did not get out of the room. He chased her up to her room where he flung her on to the bed and made her beat herself with her own hands. She ran off home and returned the next day to encounter more trouble.

Anne Boomer, the nurse, had arrived from Lewisham for a visit and found her mistress crying in her bedroom because her husband had come home in the early hours and abused her. The nurse was invited to stay for dinner and they had no sooner sat down at table than the couple started quarrelling. Mary accused Charles of drinking and neglecting his business and his family. Whereupon he reached for a knife and with the words, 'Damn me 'tis no sin to kill thee', went for his wife. The nurse tried to intervene and he flung her away and, grabbing Mary by the neck, swore he would twist her head round.

Ann Stanley, also a household servant, recounted two incidents. The first happened late on a winter's night about six months after that described above. Ann and Mistress Pepys were sitting in the dining-room, chatting by the light of a candle. Mr Pepys came up the stairs from the shop in a black mood, presumably in drink. For no apparent reason, he went over to his wife, seized the candle and burnt her face with the flame, snarling. 'Damn me, you

Bitch, I'll burn you alive'. He then went back downstairs 'rayling' and later reappeared and drew a knife on her and threw some tobacco pipes at her. When Ann Stanley tried to come between them, he threatened her with an andiron. At last 'with much adoe' they persuaded him to go to bed.

On another occasion he came home about midnight and Ann Stanley led him, with a lighted candle, up to the bedchamber, where Mary was already in bed. He usually slept downstairs, sharing a room with his boy, or lay alone. Tonight was to be different.

Charles reeled into the room and, on seeing Mary, cried: 'Damn me, you bitch, are you gott into Bed! You will not stay there long.'

He pulled her out of bed and started hitting her; she screamed and her friend, Elizabeth Newton, who was staying the night, came running up. The two women tried to get him off as he was pulling, pinching and biting Mary. Charles then made Mary sit on the edge of the bed without shoes or stockings while he lit and smoked a pipe of tobacco. When he had finished he broke it into pieces and flung them at her. The servants took to hiding knives, candlesticks and pipes from him after this.

Mary often had Elizabeth Newton spend the night in Lombard Street for company and protection. One night there was a particularly bad fight and Charles drew his sword on his terrified spouse. He then went off to the St John's Head tavern and came home with the landlord. Whereupon Mrs Pepys fled to Blossoms Inn.

Sickened by his drinking, violence and meanness (she often had to send out to her mother for food) Mary finally left him and went home to her mother, coming back under cover of darkness to take her clothes.

The men's tale presents a rather different version of events. Charles's witnesses were local merchants, mainly involved in the wine and tobacco trade. Pepys, they agree, 'is of a kind, affable and courteous temper' showing particular kindness to his wife, who deserted him quite unreasonably and refused to sleep with him. He has had a difficult time since the fire and is badly in debt, largely because of Mary's extravagance and insistence that he buy the family a country residence in Islington. After promising to be kind to Charles's children she broke 'the grisle' of her fourteen-year-old stepdaughter's nose and threatened to murder the toddler if she was brought back from the wet-nurse in the country.

She has a vicious tongue and is continually abusing Charles, wishing that 'he might rott with the plague' and expressing her desire to see him go a-begging. A barmaid says that she has seen his face badly scratched by his wife and a local writing clerk claims that Mary had a friend, 'the Captain' who was going to murder Charles for her.

Who is to be believed? Witnesses would regularly take bribes and the evidence in these sorts of suits was notoriously biased and contradictory. Reading between the lines, it seems likely that Mr Pepys, of a volatile nature, was thrown into a passion of anxiety and despair by the fire and his money worries. As men have done since time began, and certainly still do, he took to the bottle and worked out his anger on his spouse. And, as women have done since time began, and certainly still do, she took him back. The action was dropped on condition that he behave himself in future. Were screams ever heard again over that tobacconist's shop in Lombard Street?

An eighteenth-century society divorce

A hundred years later a flamboyant divorce case swept through the Consistory Court, accompanied by the daily fanfare of newspapers as far away as India and swollen by a whole battery of suits in other courts – Chancery, King's Bench, Common Pleas, the Arches, the High Court of Delegates. Again a wife was suing for separation on grounds of cruelty, which was quite a rarity by now. Most of the actions in the property-conscious eighteenth century were brought by husbands against their adulterous wives. This couple are much higher up the social scale than the tobacconist and his wife, and there is infinitely more at stake financially. Nevertheless, the patterns of beatings and burnings are remarkably similar, not only to what happened in the Pepys household but also to what is reported in the tabloid press of today.

Some 30 miles north of London, tucked away in a still remote and rural green fold of Hertfordshire, stands a fine old brick stately home with the air of a doll's house about it. It was here, at St Paul's Walden Bury, where the Queen Mother grew up, that an antecedent of hers – the heiress who put the Bowes into Bowes-Lyon – suffered the agonies of her second marriage.

Just inside the front door is a portrait of a plump-faced, pale, unattractive woman with a high pile of unflattering headdress and a little brown and white dog at her skirts. It is Mary Bowes, 9th Countess of Strathmore, who married John Lyon, Earl of Strathmore in the very year the house was built, 1767. She was fairly soon widowed and, by all accounts, set up a lively, sociable card-playing establishment in their house in Grosvenor Square. A very short-sighted, intellectual girl, a botanist of some distinction, she was not without some physical charms. Jessé Foot, a surgeon who later cashed in on the part he had played in the scandal and dashed off a quick best-seller on the subject, noted her loose, elegant dress, her 'uncommonly fine breast' as she 'glowed with all the warmth of a gay widow'. Her greatest attraction was, however, her income of £20,000 a year.

An Irish adventurer by the name of Andrew Robinson Stoney secured Mary's hand in marriage. The couple produced two children, adding to the three boys and two girls she had from the Earl. Stoney took the names Bowes and used his wife's money to further his political career, standing for Parliament. In 1786, the Countess started to struggle free of the marriage; three years later a couple of months before the Bastille was stormed, the case was concluded.

The daring adventurer's exploits, the kidnappings, the sex, the beatings, the lawsuits, the duels, the 'blood' and, above all, the wealth and high profile of the protagonists, made the case the talk of London and Madras for many a season. It was such a good story that Thackeray used it as a basis for his novel *Barry Lyndon*, published fifty years later. But it was only in the 'cozy nook near St Paul's' that the refinements of matrimonial torture were dissected and aired. 'In the Commons', wrote Jessé Foot, 'the proofs must be made out so plain, that the most minute circumstances must appear.'

Stoney Bowes was a charmer, with small, sparkling eyes, fair bushy eye-brows and a prominent hooked nose. He lisped and spoke softly and was always laughing. His first wife, an heiress, had died of a broken heart, having been systematically provoked and brutalised. On one occasion he had shut her naked in a small cupboard for three days.

At thirty-two he was free and spent his time gaming, cock-fighting and frequenting the turf and the clubs of St James's on the look out for another heiress to finance him. He chose the Dowager Countess of Strathmore and stirred up attacks on her character in the press to put her current lover off, then staged a duel (using redcurrant jelly for blood) in defence of her good name with the editor of the 'offending' paper. She was seduced by the performance and the lover was paid off with £12,000. In January 1777 Stoney and Mary were married and he proceeded to squander her fortune, indulge in sexual exploits with servant girls and beat his wife as a punishment for her very existence.

Stoney Bowes. From *The Lives of Andrew Robinson Bowes Esq. and the Countess of Strathmore* (1820), by Jessé Foot. (British Library)

Mary Bowes, 9th Countess of Strathmore. (Courtesy of the Hon. Simon Bowes-Lyon)

Duel or farce? Eighteenth-century engraving: 'The Duellists'. (The Trustees of the British Museum)

When Jessé Foot went out to St Paul's Walden Bury to innoculate their baby son, Mary was a changed woman, pale and apprehensive, always looking over her shoulder and indicating her extreme agitation by a rhythmic movement of her lower jaw.

The marriage was eight years old when it came under the scrutiny of the Civilians; one year older than the Pepys liaison when it foundered. If Charles Pepys was reluctant, for whatever reason, to lose his wife, Stoney Bowes was frantic to keep his. Mary had a fortune and mansions all over the country; on their marriage he was given a personal income of £10,000 a year. So desperate was he that he organised a gang of ruffians, including a pair known as Doctor Medecin and Four Eyes, to kidnap her when she was shopping in Oxford Street. Those protecting or supporting her he had 'arrested', procuring a stack of blank arrest warrants from a corrupt constable. When it was all over the Countess, deranged from her sufferings, put together a scrap-book of revenge. It still exists today, and in it is stuck one of the blank warrants which fluttered around inside the coach into which the kidnappers bundled her.

The coach went like the wind to the bottom of Highgate Hill where Stoney got on board. At Barnet a post-chaise and four were waiting and the party drove hell-bent for Doncaster, where they changed horses and set off for the Bowes's northern seat, Streatlam Castle. There Stoney tried to get Mary to sign a paper to stop the divorce but she refused and he took her off to his lawyer's office in Darlington, where a rescue party of her supporters found her.

While all over the country people sang *The Escape Ballad:*

Ye pimps and ye bullies of mighty renown
The pride of each brothel and boast of the town,
Thro' the realms of old Drury re-echo my song
And praise the Great St*n*y your Captain prolong
Derry down, down derry down

the evidence was still to be sifted in the Consistory, the Arches, the Delegates and King's Bench.

There is no doubt that Stoney's witnesses were bribed wholesale; everybody said so and much of the evidence just does not ring true. Nevertheless his defence was cunningly contrived, making the best of the material at his disposal; the Countess was clearly an odd character. Jessé Foot reckoned that there was not much to choose between the two of them. Neither Stoney nor the Countess had, he wrote, 'received one single check from any compunctious visitings of nature . . . both of them appeared as if they had been taken from a land not yet in a state of Civilization, and dropped by accident where they had been found.'

The case brought the usual parade of servants to Doctors' Commons. The relationships between master and mistress and the staff who were continually in their company, attending to their every physical need and acting as confidants, has no modern parallel. The interdependence of servant and master, and more particularly maid and mistress, could produce an unhealthy closenesss, often of a love–hate nature. 'The misrepresentation of servants', said Stoney, 'were often the ruin of the most respectable families.' Let us see what they said about him.

The leading character on Lady Strathmore's side was her lady's maid, Mary Morgan. Her evidence starts with an account of a trip made to France in 1784. Stoney and the Countess, with Morgan in attendance, went to Paris with Lady Anna Maria Bowes, one of Mary's daughters by the Earl. (This was an attempt on Stoney's part to get the Strathmore children under his control, and the Bowes family, wary of what was going on, had started proceedings in Chancery to get them away from their mother.) In the coach he contradicted 'almost everything she said', kept slyly pinching her and every time he caught her looking at something out of the window he would pull the blinds down.

When they got to the Hotel de Luxembourg, Morgan went to attend to her mistress, who was sharing a room with the teenage Lady Anna Maria, and found the former standing with her head against a chest of drawers sobbing and bleeding copiously. The husband, in a transparent attempt to cover up what he had been doing, said to Morgan: 'That woman can take no care of herself and has let the wind blow open one of the doors and by that means run a black Pin into her.'

Whilst the family stayed in Paris, Stoney burnt his wife with candles and stuck a pen-nib through her tongue. He would summon her into his room for regular beatings for no reason; sometimes because she 'did not weare her Bonnet forward enough over her face'.

Morgan next recounts an incident which happened at St Paul's Walden Bury. Mary Bowes, like her royal descendants, was inordinately fond of dogs and had, apparently, invited a friend to dinner and suggested that she should bring her pet dog. Morgan, summoned by the Countess's bell, went up to her bedchamber and found her bruised and weeping. Her husband had administered the usual physical punishment and then made her kneel and swear on the Bible that she would never again invite a dog to the house.

One night in the Grosvenor Square house Morgan was undressing Lady Anna Maria when the Countess came in and asked if she would light her into the drawing-room to fetch some papers. The girl objected, so Mary went in the dark, passing through the dressing-room where Stoney was. The maid heard her master go into the drawing-room and the next sound was a noise 'like a Pair of fire trugs falling with great force'. For half an hour the couple were in the dark room together. Morgan and the fifteen-year-old daughter could hear the Countess's screams as he roared out that he would teach her to 'be beat without crying out'.

Stoney used various means to keep his wife confined, telling her that she was too slovenly in her dress to be seen in public. Morgan says she did not 'have any great Taste in Dress' but was certainly decent. He would order the knocker to be tied up at their town house so the neighbours would think she was ill.

When the Countess finally planned her escape she asked Morgan to go to the Lord Chancellor on her behalf, presumably to obtain a writ of *supplicavit* for protection.

Dorothy Stevenson, a young nurserymaid whom Stoney had raped and made pregnant, told the examiner that her master was 'cruel, savage and abandonned'. He kept the mistress short of clothes: 'she had scarcely a shift or a pair of stockings', and would hit, kick and pinch her if he considered she was making too much noise playing with her little boy. She remembered an altercation which ended with him trying to 'cram her into a cupboard'.

The Countess was taken ill one evening at the Bury and went up to her dressing-room with the nurserymaid, where she had a fit. Dorothy ran downstairs to fetch the apothecary who had been dining with them. Stoney refused to let the guest go up to his wife and went up himself, firmly shutting the door of the dressing-room. Screams were heard and the next day Mary could hardly lift her arms, they were so sore and stiff.

The nurserymaid used to eat at a side table in the same room as her employers and was a first-hand witness when it came to the virtually inevitable dining row. On a May afternoon in 1784, the Bowes were at table and Stoney was reprimanding his wife for walking in the park without his permission. He threw a dish of hot potatoes in her face and then stood over her while she ate them 'till she was quite sick', flinging a glass of wine in her face to 'wash them down'. Although she uttered not a word, he took a large table knife to her throat and threatened to cut it if she spoke. After the meal was over Dorothy was ordered from the room. When she saw her mistress later, with a bruised face and bleeding ear, she asked if he had hurt her. The Countess replied that she 'durst not say'.

To grant a separation on grounds of cruelty, there had to be repeated, unjustified physical abuse. Stoney's case was that his wife was mad and bad, a drinker, a drug taker, promiscuous and an inadequate, neglectful mother. All of which was, firstly, justification for his violence and, secondly, reason for not believing her allegations. She did take laudanum, and who can wonder? She was eccentric and probably did prefer pets to children. He claimed, moreover, that she was persuaded to leave him under the malign and overbearing influence of the maid Morgan. Her bruises and burns were the result of her clumsiness; she was careless and accident prone. There was a deal of fuss about 'a contrivance of wire' over the fireplace in her dressing-room which he had apparently devised to prevent her catching her headdress on fire when she was reading. According to her daughter she frequently did this, as she read a lot by candle-light and was very short-sighted. The fact that he had procured the contrivance was supposed to show his extreme care for her welfare.

There came to the Commons to support Stoney abortionists, prostitutes and a whole crew of unsavoury characters, including those of the servants whom he had been successful in bribing. One of the maids who testified for the Countess told the examiner that Stoney had tried to buy her silence in a coffee house in the Spring Garden. The butler and a female relative of his appeared. The former was rather cagey in his evidence, but the woman was more forthcoming. She testified to her mistress's clumsiness and tendency to hurt herself and confirmed that she neglected her children. The young Earl of Strathmore was heard to say that he 'wished he was a cat that his Mamma would love him'.

The surgeon who was called to tell tales about the Countess's sexual activities strangely failed to remember whether she came to him just before her second marriage to have an abortion (as a result of her liaison with an East India Company nabob called Gray) or whether it was because she was 'irregular in her monthly discharge'. The lawyers showed him exhibit A, a very odd letter which still exists, purporting to have a note on it in the Countess's hand making reference to the abortion. He had no opinion of whether or not it was Mary's hand, but was quite clear that she preferred cats and dogs to her children. The abortion story was almost certainly made up; Morgan, when asked if her mistress had had Gray's baby after her marriage to Stoney, denied it and said it was a seven-month baby.

William Davis, a middle-aged man with a St James's address who had first met Stoney at dinner in a Bond Street tavern nine years earlier, was perhaps a high-living friend of Stoney's who would be grateful for cash in hand to pay his gambling debts. This witness had observed a happy marriage, a caring, loving husband and a wife distressed only by the unkindness of her children. He had, however, heard that the Countess's affair with Mr Gray hastened her first husband's death. The East India Company nabob was not her only entertainment; there was also George Walker the footman, with whom, he had heard, she is yet again 'in criminal conversation'!

Stoney's last fling was an abortive appeal to the High Court of Delegates on the grounds of his wife's affair with the gardener at their house at Gibside.

In the end, the Countess got her freedom; Stoney was put in prison for kidnapping her and the Arches ordered him to pay £300 a year alimony and costs. The lawyers had good pickings; in July 1791 the papers reported that Lady Strathmore's proctors were owed £1,187 for proceedings in the Commons. But, for the Countess, it was no happy ending. The scrap-book is witness to her obsessive desire for revenge and reassurance. Every newspaper report of the trouble in which Stoney subsequently found himself is carefully pasted in with appropriate comments. And in September 1791, Mary noted a paragraph in a paper which mentioned that she was at Weymouth at the same time as their Majesties and that she was in favour with them.

The Countess predeceased Stoney, dying in April 1800, just eleven years after the divorce decree, and was buried in Westminster Abbey in her wedding dress. Stoney lived on with another woman, having managed to recover enough property to procure a living income.

Stoney Bowes was a fortune hunter. After the marriage Lady Strathmore had (under duress, as she later claimed) revoked the trust deed which made sure that all her property remained in her own hands. In 1785 she tried to reverse the situation by going to Chancery and the case was referred to Common Pleas who declared this later revocation invalid. It was, says Jessé Foot, after this that the trouble really started between the couple. No wonder he beat her when she went into the drawing-room after papers!

But had Stoney behaved lovingly and decently towards her, he could have enjoyed her wealth to his heart's content. The evidence given to the Consistory suggested that the physical abuse started soon after the wedding, and was the cause, rather than the occasion, of her attempts to reassume control of her estate. Who knows what motivated Stoney in his wife-beating. Perhaps he was humiliated as a child or sorely beaten by someone himself. Perhaps his mother or nurse had sickened him of female domination and, while he sought a woman to keep him, he felt compelled to punish her for the power she had over him.

We will leave the couple with an epitaph which Lady Strathmore penned for her hated spouse:

> Here rests, who never rested before
> The most ambitious of men
> . . . rose by deep hypocrisy

To honours which Nature had forbid,
And riches he wanted taste to enjoy.
He saw no faults in himself,
Nor any worth in others.
He was an enemy of mankind;
Deceitful to his friends,
Ungrateful to his benefactors,
Cringeing to his superiors,
And tyrannical to his dependants.

'Clamours of murder at midnight'. A cheated whore attacks her customer as the madam pours a 'pot of pisse' on to his head (*c.*1550). (Reproduced in *London, the Synfulle Citie* (1990) by E J Burford)

3

At the Court of Scolds

Neighbours in slander actions

FROM THE BEDCHAMBER and the dressing-room where the matrimonial agonies of our ancestors were played out, let us move into a more public arena and take a look at some of the jealousies and revenges between neighbours which excercised the ordinary inhabitants of early modern London. In doing so we will be going, with the litigants and witnesses who came to the courts, into the darkest corners of the capital, following Ben Jonson's vice, Iniquity, who went from the top of St Paul's to 'survey the suburbs':

> Down Petticoat-lane and up the Smock-alleys,
> To Shoreditch and Whitechapel, and so to St Kathern's,
> To drink with the Dutch there, and take forth their patterns.

The scolds are to be found in murky passages and rat-infested courtyards, where link boys dare not light the way, in noisy alehouses and overcrowded tenements.

Our route is along summer streets, stinking of garbage and sewage, overhung with ruinous half-timbered lodging houses, 'pestered', as the topographer Stow put it, with shops and market stalls, choked with smoke from foundries, breweries and starch works. Here are the 'meaner sort', their faces flushed and swollen with drink, their demeanour anxious. They are constantly on the watch for trouble. Pockets are picked where 'impudent Harlots' in 'Antick Dresses' with 'Painted faces and whorish Insinuations', with 'poxd Bodies' cause tumult. Signboards are pulled down, windows smashed and there are 'clamours of murder . . . at Midnight'.

The acrimony between husbands and wives, spawned of love turned to hate, unrequited passion, rejection and betrayal, can almost be matched by what passes when neighbours who are living in close proximity and harsh conditions fall out, especially if they are prostitutes competing for trade. In the sixteenth and seventeenth centuries the courts at the Commons conducted what might seem to us a strangely lively trade in slander actions between members of the labouring classes.

The witnesses were required to repeat, as nearly as they could, the exact words which were spoken when neighbour slandered neighbour, putting them into context. Some of them were vague in their recollections, like Grizell Waters, a servant girl who came before the Consistory in 1679. She thought the event under consideration happened perhaps in June or July, 'as she taketh it – Green Beanes being then newly come in'. Most of them were not in the way of keeping an exact account of affairs; hardly any of the women were literate. When they gave the court examiner their version of events they rattled on in their everyday speech. What they said was tightened and tidied up by the clerks who wrote it down in the deposition books, but it is still possible to hear snatches of three- and four-hundred-year-old quarrels, to get a flavour of those long dead hatreds between angry bawds, apprentices and serving girls, labourers and nurse-keepers. Here are annals of the poor as full and lively as any courtiers' tittle-tattle or accounts of more prosperous lives preserved in the diaries and letters of gentlemen.

It was once the fashion to regard pre-industrial society in this country with a nostalgic eye; to see an idyll of Merry England with peaceful townsfolk at ease in their lath and plaster dwellings and contented farm workers ploughing their furrows. There was maypole dancing for the young, neat almshouses with herb gardens for the old, and villagers tended their flocks in a spirit of pastoral co-operation. In the days of lace caps and clean, country water, the benign squire and parson watched over their flock. Everyone knew his or her place and was secure and relaxed. For those who fell on hard times there was always poor relief; 'Hang sorrow and cast away care', they sang, 'the Parish is bound to find us!'

These days historians of the early modern period see our ancestors in angry mood, 'apt to turn every pretence and colour of grievance into uproar and seditious mutiny'. A picture is painted of a cold, hostile society, with jumpy, suspicious, irritable people ever ready to attack, with malice and fear in their hearts. The reinterpretation is partly ascribable to the exploration of the records of the courts of law, lay and ecclesiastical. Violent crime seems to have been on the increase from the late sixteenth century, litigation was rife; you only had to take a stroll round Westminster and the legal quarters of town to see swarms of folk with their lawyers clinging to them like ivy. During the law terms, brothels might charge five times as much as they did in the vacations. People from all ranks took advantage of the waves of moral purge brought in with religious reforms to wreak vengeance on neighbours with whom they had fallen out.

Too much stress can, perhaps, be laid on the turbulence of society; writing history from legal records may be compared to reconstructing modern British society from the pages of the *Sun*. But it was a disturbing era and, before going out into the streets to listen to what was said in the brawls there, it is worth considering, first, something of the background to the anger voiced by ordinary Londoners and, second, why they bothered to sue.

Between the Reformation and the Glorious Revolution was a time of upheaval. The monasteries were closed, the roods taken down from the churches, candles snuffed out and comforting saints banished. One day there would be one queen and the next, another. Witches rode and village streets rang with the cacophony of rough music and charivari as nervous communities fell back on the old ways of restoring domestic order. If you spoke out

'Rough music and charivari'. The 'skimmington ride' shown here was a public expression of ridicule at nagging wives or unfaithful husbands. Detail from Samuel Butler's *Hudibras,* engraved by William Hogarth (1726)

of turn you might find yourself in some human bonfire. Then came the 'starvation years' of the 1590s and 1620s, when the population was rising fast. Inflation and enclosure combined to bring severe economic distress. Real wages halved in the second half of the sixteenth century and continued to drop for another twenty or thirty years after the turn of the century. Bands of vagrants roamed the land in search of work. The ecclesiastical social security system had all but collapsed, and the Government issued orders to try and boost charitable giving in church. Books were published listing the different categories of beggars, so the unwary might be prepared for them. There was 'Tom o' Bedlam' who had been turned out on to the streets from the madhouse, 'seekers for glimmer of light' who had lost everything by fire, and many others. Jennings, a versatile Elizabethan beggar, did a good imitation of epilepsy. In 1601 legislation was introduced which imposed a poor rate on householders.

There were, however, for all sorts and conditions, ways of making money which had not been available before. A variety of new trades and industries were springing up and any unemployed and landless labourer might board ship at Wapping or Bristol and come back a year later from Virginia with his pockets jingling. Twenty thousand pounds can easily be made from the sale of bottled ale, says Ben Jonson's character, Meercraft. He also has a scheme to market a home-grown raisin drink 'as true as the wines of France' at half the price. With the profits he makes from that and the mass-production of toothpicks, he will return to Italy, leaving the 'smoke of England' for ever. *Plus ça change* . . .

For women, prostitution was the obvious way to get rich quick and there were big profits to be made at 5*s.* or 2*s.* 6*d.* a night. One lady, whom we shall meet later, charged a guinea.

After generations at the plough, many a 'Meercraft family' took a leap up the social ladder. James I sold knighthoods to the *nouveaux riches* and the College of Arms did a good trade in badges of respectability for those who had made their pile. The ancient genealogies sported by many a noble family date from this time, when some member made a fortune in wool dealing or property speculation, buying up cheap monastic land, and 'lived like a gentleman thereby'.

The dislocation of society which started in the mid-sixteenth century came to a head with the collapse of good neighbourliness during the Civil War, while the proliferation of strange sects and cults set men and women against one another. Even after the Monarchy was restored in 1660 and the Act of Indemnity and Oblivion was passed, it took some generations for the wounds to heal.

The general spirit of agitation and competition, which was reflected in the activities in law courts all over the country, was as nothing compared to what happened in London. The Earl of Clarendon, Charles II's Lord Chancellor, described it as the 'sink of ill-humours of this kingdom'. Between 1600 and 1700 the population of the 'flower of cities all' may well have doubled. The swelling of the 'great wen' had started perhaps fifty years before that; lack of reliable statistics make it difficult to assess how much. Suffice it to say that perhaps as many as 80 per cent of the 'Londoners' who came to the Commons to give evidence in the reign of Elizabeth were country bred. Drawn to the capital in search of the work which was no longer available on the land, they swarmed into the liberties and out-parishes.

The little medieval walled city was bursting at the seams. In spite of building restrictions, houses were springing up everywhere. The father of the poet Middleton, who died in 1586, was a bricklayer who made enough money to buy himself a coat of arms. The easier route, rather than risk prosecution, was to patch up the old; crumbling mansions were converted into lodging houses and furnished rooms rented out. James Burbage, the father of Shakespeare's leading man, converted a Shoreditch barn, which had belonged to Holywell Priory, into a number of small dwellings. Every part of existing buildings was used and many householders let out their cellars to shopkeepers.

The eastern suburbs filled up the most; it was there the vice Iniquity went on his flying survey. St Dunstan's, Stepney, which served most of the three square miles east of Aldgate, became one of the busiest at buryings and marryings of any church in the kingdom. Along the highways from the Tower to Wapping, from Aldgate to beyond Whitechapel, from Bishopsgate up to the village of Kingsland, small houses were pushed in, covering the open spaces.

On the other side of the City, the newcomers flooded into the tenements of St Giles, St Martins and St Clement Danes. Brothels, gaming houses and all sorts of drinking establishments appeared around Drury Lane and Covent Garden. Chick Lane and Long Lane in West Smithfield became dangerous places to visit unaccompanied.

It was a world of strangers, a 'bed-sitter land' of predominantly young folk, where family support was far away. There were foreigners, too. Dutch and French, escaping from religious persecution, settled in the liberties and suburbs and undercut the home rag trade. They 'sett women and Maydes' to work, complained the Elizabethan Weavers' Company, and go 'hawking upp and downe the Cittye daye by daye, and from Shoppe to Shoppe, offering all kinds of work to sell'. When the big influx of Huguenots arrived, after the Revocation of the Edict of Nantes in 1685, the vicar of Whitechapel said they were 'the very offal of the earth'. We shall hear later what the women of Wapping thought about the Flemings.

To the young girl up from the shires, rumbling towards the City on the carrier's cart, with her small bundle of belongings and hopes of finding a

A 'young girl up from the shires'. Detail from the frontispiece to Paul Scarron's *Roman Comique* (1676), engraved by W Fairthorne. (Cambridge University Library)

place with a kind family, it must have been a bewildering and frightful prospect. Perhaps the plague bell was tolling out its terrible message, as it did with sickening regularity in the late months of hot summers. Her mother would probably have warned her of the dangers and, no doubt, told her to protect her good name if she wanted to make a decent match. Some said that nothing but a *subpoena* would induce them to go to London, where all you could expect was a disfiguring dose of the pox. Your babies were more likely to die than they were at home and the chances of a marriage lasting long enough for anyone to get the seven-year itch were less. But beggars can't be choosers and never could.

Did she and her fellows take their mothers' warnings to heart? Were the servant girls, midwives, hairdressers, lodging house keepers, silk throwsters and nurse-keepers, who took themselves in their droves to the London church courts in defamation suits, really so desperate to protect their reputations that they were willing to risk losing two years' wages on the enterprise? Was the concern for what Wycherley's Lady Fidget called her 'dear, dear honour' something which filtered down from the gentry and afflicted even the barmaids in Whitechapel alehouses? Or was there some hidden agenda? If it got around that you were plying the oldest trade, there might, of course, be unpleasant consequences. You might be tied to the cart's tail or whipped. In times of moral purge there were worse punishments. But would anybody seriously believe you were a prostitute, just because they heard some angry neighbour calling out 'you whore'?

Slander suits had always taken up a good proportion of the time in the church courts. They accounted for nearly half the business of the London Commissary Court in 1514. Women were always active participants, for obvious reasons. The jurisdiction of those courts was over defamatory words which impuned the victim's moral character. If a man was called a 'cankered curl' by the woman next door, his recourse was to the king's court. If he was accused of dishonesty in his dealings and his livelihood was thereby jeopardised, he could seek the protection of the common law. If, however, his wife was told repeatedly and in front of witnesses, that she was a whore, then only the church could offer a remedy. In theory a prostitute could have sued at common law for the protection of her trade if someone had called her a 'poxey whore', but none ever did.

There was a steep rise in slander actions, starting in the sixteenth century and peaking towards the end of the seventeenth, not by any means confined to the capital. All over England women were suing 'for words'. In the Chester Consistory defamations quadrupled between 1544 and 1594. For the lawyers at the Commons, business was brisk in the 1620s and 1630s with suits coming into the two bishop's courts and the archdeacon's courts. Between 1637 and 1640 the Consistory's litigious business was about 80 per cent slander, and it was much the same in the two other courts. By the 1680s there was even more.

An increase in litigation and legal activity of all sorts was a feature of the period, as we have noticed, something which might be expected from a society which was moving into capitalism. Small businessmen, manufacturers, retailers, merchants and entrepreneurs needed a mechanism for securing the payment of debts. More economic activity meant more legal activity. With land being bought and sold more often than it had been before, there were more likely to be disputes over titles. All that is readily understood and it may be that the rise in defamations was just quarrelsome neighbours getting on the legal bandwagon. Rather than a sign of any growing preoccupation with honour, the slander boom was perhaps another reflection of the crisis of order noticed by historians. In the prevailing climate of anxiety, there was more scolding going on than there had been before, and the church courts, with their new high profile, born of the religious reforms, were being used to end quarrels which might previously have been settled by private arbitration or even fizzled out of their own accord.

The language of abuse is largely sexual, and any squabble in the market-place or on the doorstep, over some trifling incident, might blow up into something which might be readily taken to the court of conscience. In the spats and brawls which were subjected to the scrutiny of the Civilians, the same insults came rolling off the tongue time and time again. These days pub conversations, even those without acrimony, are heavily larded with variations on the word 'fucking'. In the fifteenth century the favoured adjective was 'whoreson'. When Shakespeare wrote the dialogue for the young Prince Hal and his low drinking companions, he used what was by then, an archaic term of abuse: 'Thou whoreson, obscene, greasy tallow chandler', 'Thou whoreson, impudent, embossed fellow', says the Prince to Falstaff. Listen to Isabella Newport, brought before the Commissary in 1492:

> I met Newport and had the hooreson by the face . . . and pushed him
> into the dyche [Houndsditch] . . . the bald hooreson Cokkold wer
> hangyd than he should be my husband . . . I tryst that I shall fynde sum
> goode fellowe that, for my sake, ether even or morowe, shalt make hym
> to pysse above his gyrdlsted [waist].

In the 1680s nearly every one of the many slander suits in the Consistory were brought by women. As we have seen, this is partly because of the nature of the language of swearing. A couple engaged in a feud with a neighbour could use the 'scandalous words' spoken against the wife as a way into court, and many did. Some suits were cooked up by a group of locals to punish a persistent trouble-maker, with men involved as much as their spouses. Nevertheless, there is no doubt that many women were active at 'affrays' on their own account, as litigants, witnesses and brawlers. The ordinary women of early modern London, like their more elevated sisters, were a tough and independent bunch. A favourite theme for playwrights in the seventeenth century was the 'new woman' and 'the world turned upside down', with the woman taking the man's role. Joseph Swetnam's *Arraignment of Lewd, Idle,*

Froward and Inconstant Women went into ten editions between 1615 and 1634. A Southampton Leet jury noticed in 1603 the 'manifold number of scolding women that there be in this town'.

Scolds and whores tended to be bracketed together by contemporaries; they shared the same humiliating punishment and were often referred to in the same breath. Prostitution was, as we have seen, on the increase and it is not chance that the areas of London listed in a 1622 proclamation against brothels are exactly those which keep reappearing in the accounts of slander suits: Cowcross, Smithfield, St John Street, Clerkenwell, Shoreditch, Petticoat Lane, Charterhouse Liberty and Norton Folgate. The Doctors of the courts Christian were, ironically, often called upon to arbitrate when 'impudent harlots' fell out among themselves.

Bitches snarl and dogs bite. No man from the male brothel in Beech Lane seems to have taken any of his rivals to the Commons. These were violent times. Ben Jonson ran a fellow player through with a sword and Shakespeare was bound over to keep the peace. Richard Gough noted ten homicides in the village of Myddle from the mid- to late seventeenth century. What happened when Thomas Newton had been drinking all day in a Myddle alehouse must have been typical of incidents all over the country, especially in the years following the Civil War. He got into a slanging match with someone 'using that rude, damning language which he had learned when he was a soldier'. The protagonists went for their weapons, a pike and a sword. One was killed and the other arraigned at the Assizes.

While their mates resorted to fisticuffs, or worse, women were more inclined, as William Heale remarked in his *Apology for Women* (1603) to express their rage and misery with the 'lavish of their tongues'. Witches were well known for it. A spate of witch trials swept through Europe at this time; many of the spells were cast when women fell out about the exchange of goods and, almost without exception, the case featured women with ready, sharp and angry tongues. The lawyers defending a Scottish 'witch' in Eyemouth referred to 'a sort of Railing and Flyting [quarrelling] which is common to women stirred up by their neighbours'.

The world we are about to enter, then, is one that simmers with resentment. It is also awash with drink. Ale and wine were cheap and sold everywhere. Drink oiled the wheels of society at all levels and, for the poor, it provided an escape from a hostile environment. The women we will meet drank quite as much as the men, going to taverns and alehouses for a pint or more of white wine, their usual tipple. Joan Haughton, said a witness at St Paul's in 1627, persuaded two men to 'gett wine to be made drunke . . . and laidest spewing at the Three Cuppes beyond the Shamballs . . . near Newgate market upon a Bedd and was then drunk as a Bitch'.

The drinking houses were social centres where foremen paid wages to their labourers, sailors were recruited, the local mail was delivered, and men and women conducted business with their lawyers and scriveners. Eating out was very usual; some East London ditchers involved in a probate suit in the 1590s all took their breakfast in a victualling house. In Pepys's day there were numerous 'ordinaries' where you could get a cheap set meal.

A good deal of time was spent chatting on street corners and on doorsteps; gossip flew around and, although there were many dark corners where you could hide, life there was still a much more public affair than it is now. The notion of 'common fame' was alive and well in the courts and people knew their neighbours' business. The Shoreditch beadle, called to discredit a witness in the Consistory in 1681, said that he knew every householder in the parish and the tailor in question was 'noe such man'.

Let us go now and hear something of that 'railing and flyting', and, if it is not as entertaining or well tuned as that of the Falstaff gang in the Boar's Head in Eastcheap, of Ben Jonson's market women at Bartholomew Fair, or in the taverns of Restoration comedy, remember that what is said in an altercation in the *Queen Vic* or the *Rovers Return* bears little comparison to real life. What was repeated at the Commons is interesting because it is the authentic voice of angry ancestors taken for the most part from the bottom ranks of society. If the words are updated a little, it does not sound very different from what passes today. Consider what Isabella Newport, who pushed her husband into Houndsditch 500 years ago, would say if she were alive now: 'I met Newport and had the f***r by the face, and pushed him into the canal . . . the f***in' bald c***t.'

At the court of the Archdeacon of London in Elizabethan times

In 1566 the Protestant Queen has been on the throne for eight years and the country is beginning to settle down into the long reign of petticoat government. The political and religious turn and turn about that took place in the short period when Elizabeth's brother and then her sister were ruling have left ordinary folk wary.

The doctors of Civil Law are still at their old headquarters in Paternoster Row, just near St Paul's; they did not move to Knightrider Street until 1568. In those days the Archdeacon's Court sat a stone's throw away in Christchurch, Newgate, the largest parish church in London. It was part of the dissolved Greyfriars' monastery and stood to the north-west of the cathedral, just outside the City gate. Among others buried there was the Holy Maid of Kent, burnt in 1534 for preaching against Henry VIII's marriage to Anne Boleyn.

It was an insalubrious spot. To the south of the great church was a market place with butchers' and poulterers' stalls, slaughterhouses and the stocks where drunks were punished. Adjoining was the orphans' school, Christ's Hospital, where many of the children had been 'taken off the dung hill', and nearby was the dilapidated medieval prison. All that is left of Christchurch

London approached from Islington. Engraved by Waller. (The Guildhall Library, London)

today is the Wren spire and a shell. The consistorial place where the court met is covered with roses.

In the autumn and winter of 1566–7 there came from Islington a group of people in the matter of an affray. Islington was a large parish, extending north from the City boundary at Clerkenwell. Famous for its ducking pond, it was a favourite spot for apprentices to take their girls for a day's outing. Its open fields were a haunt for robbers and vagrants. In the 1580s the Recorder said that the brick kilns at Islington were 'the chief nursery of . . . evil people'.

One day, towards the end of October, reported the innkeeper in the group, a Gloucester-born man, he was in the backyard of the baker who lived next door, when he heard the sound of 'chiding in the street'. He went to find out what was going on and, seeing Margaret James in a state of agitation, asked what was amiss. 'It is about a learinge hoore whoe stareth at me, yender, out of the door', said she, pointing at Elizabeth North, who was standing in the doorway opposite.

A young bricklayer's wife from Wiltshire, who happened to be in the street, heard Margaret say that Elizabeth was 'an arrant whore' and 'that if he wold not occupy her . . . she wold occupy him'. She did not know who 'he' was.

An aged Shropshire yeoman was blunter. He heard: 'If he wold not ryde her . . . she wold ryde him'. The world turned upside down?

The following Sunday, Margaret was publicly denounced and excommunicated by the minister during divine service in the parish church. Her husband, Clement, did not improve matters by standing up in his pew and shouting out before the assembled congregation that Elizabeth North was, indeed, a whore.

Alice Pickeringe lived down at the Vintry, by the river bank, among the great wine warehouses, some of them solid stone edifices put up in years past by merchants from Bordeaux. Whether or not she sold her favours we shall probably never know, but some of her neighbours said she did and she sued. The occasion of the uttering of the defamatory words was as follows: the neighbours, three of them, were leaning out of their respective windows, hanging washing on a line which was strung across the tenement they all occupied. As they pegged, they chatted and the subject under discussion was Alice.

Mistress Parry remarked that Alice Pickeringe was a whore and to be found in bed with Edward Godfrey. She went on in that busybody, know-all, self-righteous way that has well survived the intervening centuries: 'She hath proved herself what she ys, for she is fled away for trouble for that matter!'

Fled away she may have been, but Edward Godfrey was not, and, as Mistress Parry was speaking, she noticed his head pop up in Alice's window. 'Neighbour Parry', warned one of the other women. 'Take hede what you say, for there ys one in Pyckering's window that wyteth all that you speke!' Ann Parry bridled and replied hotly that 'She cared not' and 'would say the more . . . 'Be you there?', she called to Godfrey, 'I will say the more for it! . . . How can she [Pickering] be an honest woman when she was found in bed with thee?'

On the face of it, that was a trivial enough incident, but who knows what lay behind it. Had Alice Pickeringe perhaps been stealing Anne Parry's custom, or even her husband?

A party of shop assistants were at the Greyfriars' Church in the same session on what appears to have been an even slighter matter than the wives from the Vintry. They came from the Old Change, a street which ran north–south down the east flank of St Paul's churchyard. If the evidence taken down by the court examiner is to be believed, the tradesmen there were a bunch of nervous, volatile people; it is a tale of imagined slights and exaggerated insults. They came to court, in theory, because one of their number, Alice Kindon, was accused by one of her customers, Joan Swaldell, of slandering her good name.

There were three youngsters who had heard Alice slander Joan. They were Beatrice Bent, a sixteen-year-old from Shropshire who helped out in her landlord's armourer's shop, John Cheyney, a Lincolnshire lad, apprentice to a tailor whose shop was three doors from the Kindons, and Margaret Hughes, a girl who worked for her father, a barber.

One Tuesday in September, the young witnesses heard the sound of Alice Kindon and her husband, John, 'multiplying of words together'. They went out of their shops into the street so they could hear what passed and ascertained that the quarrel had started when Joan Swaldell, a customer, left

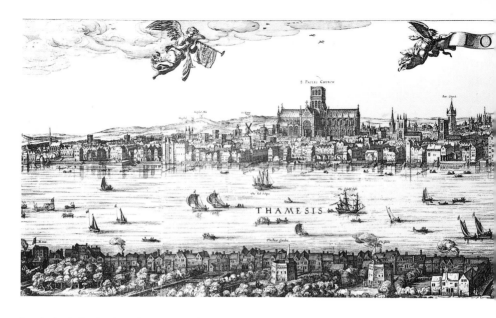

London's skyline in the early seventeenth century, dominated by the massive tower of old St Paul's Cathedral. From Nicholas Visscher's panorama (1616). (Museum of London)

the Kindon's shop, without speaking to Alice, and brushed by her husband, who was manning the stall outside, knocking his elbow.

Alice, annoyed, started on at her husband, asking him, probably not for the first time, if he intended to take her to Stourbridge Fair (the annual horse-fair), 'Yea or noe?'. 'Noe', replied he, 'For . . . I will not hire a horse for the, for it is enough for me to hire a horse for my self'.

Alice, 'very angerlie and maliciously' shouted: 'Thou will not suffer me to goe with the, but they whoore and thy harlotte, such as Swaldall's wief is, who jogged the one the elbowe as she went by, shall goe with the!', adding that she was a 'drabbe' to have ignored her and 'much other evell talk'.

A middle-aged haberdasher and an elderly innkeeper appeared for Alice Kindon, to discredit Joan's witnesses. They said that the tailor's apprentice, John Cheyney, was 'a young felowe . . . a very contensious and brablinge felowe', well known for upsetting the tailor's customers when he served on his master's stall. On one occasion in August, for instance, a serving-man had come by the shop carrying a child's fiddle. Cheyney had called out: 'Tom Fidler, lett us have a fitt of mirthe'.

For reasons which must have had more to do with the apprentice's demeanour than his words, the serving-man and his companion drew their swords. There would have been a fight had not some passers-by pacified them.

More significantly, the apprentice had upset John Kindon. As he was returning home one evening Kindon passed the house of his friend, Fardoe the grocer, and called out: 'Grocer, haste thou supped yet?' The cheeky apprentice, who was in the street, called back: 'Anon, anon!'

Kindon, outraged that 'Another man's servant should so answere him in deryision', snapped: 'Sir knave, I speke not to you, but to my neighbour'. Whereupon the apprentice, 'contrary to his duty and without respect', called back: 'It is not an hour sithens we were knaves both'.

There is no hint of what the boy had seen Kindon doing, but he rushed hastily into his master's house, before there could be any more trouble, muttering that Kindon was a 'stinking knave' and a 'coverdeick'.

There was evidently a feud going on between John Kindon and the tailor three doors away and they had been to arbitration before the suit came to the church court. Perhaps it stemmed from the bold tricks of the young apprentice or maybe its roots lay somewhere else entirely. As the wily Civilians discovered, this was far from being a simple case of an outraged woman defending her virtue. One is left wondering whether Joan Swaldell, who jogged Kindon's elbow as she left his shop, was really a scorned mistress. If so she would have been eager to join with his enemy, the tailor, to take revenge on her lover. Which of the two women, if either, got to Stourbridge Fair?

At the Bishop of London's court in the 1620s

The language used in the case of the shopkeepers of the Old Change seems mild, nursery-rhyme stuff when compared to the insults which flew back and forth in a Wapping alley some sixty years later. The Wapping case was heard before the judge of the Commissary Court which had its formal hearings at that time in St Paul's.

When the women involved in the suit took a tuppenny boat ride from Wapping to St Paul's Wharf, or trudged the two miles from home to the cathedral, it would have presented a very different aspect from the hallowed quiet of Wren's marble temple. They would have been able to see the massive Gothic pile from a long way off. Like Canary Wharf, its tower, the tallest in Christendom, rose far higher than any other building. Inside was a bustling market and meeting place, the nearest thing early modern London had to a labour exchange. The witnesses were examined in the offices of Doctors' Commons. First they had to be sworn in the cathedral itself, making their way to the Long Chapel, country folk in hob-nailed boots, most of them, whose 'heavy trot and iron stalk', the poet Middleton noticed, was wearing away the brasses in the walks.

It was in the Long Chapel that Ben Jonson's proctor character, Littlewit, performed, one of the 'pretty wits o' Paul's'. 'Every line that a proctor writes,' said another character in *Bartholomew Fair*, 'when it comes to be read out in the Bishop's court, is a long black hair, combed out of the tail of antichrist'. But then Jonson had less reason than Chaucer or Dickens to love the courts Christian; he had been persecuted by them for popish activities.

It is idle to imagine that the rougher, cruder speech of the Wapping men and women of the 1620s is a reflection of more troubled times. Rows in the Southwark stews and Tudor bawdy houses were, no doubt, as rich in crude abuse. But times *were* harder for these Wappingers than they were for the shopkeepers of the City in the 1560s. Money did not stretch as far and, as the capital sucked more and more of the poor into its industrial hinterland, London's market gardening villages became slums. A report written at the beginning of James I's reign reckoned that as many as 2,000 souls were on poor relief in some parishes.

If you set out from the Tower and walked for about half an hour in an easterly direction, past the red-light district of East Smithfield and St Katharine's, where Iniquity went drinking with the Dutch, you would find yourself in the 'sea faring end of town'. Wapping, a hamlet of Stepney, was a 'new town' at the beginning of the seventeenth century, where ships were fitted out for trips to the New World. The triangle of land jutting out into the river, with an ancient settlement on its eastern side, had been marsh until it was drained eighty years before. As the royal shipyards at Deptford expanded, so Wapping filled up with ships' carpenters, sail and ropemakers and mariners. When Henry VIII came to the throne it had been scattered islands in a reedy marsh, dotted with fishermen's boats and swans' nests, with only the cry of the moorhen to disturb the tranquil waters. Now the sky is black with masts; ale-houses, brothels and lodging houses crowd in with poky mud and weather-board cottages, hastily thrown up by developers. The sounds are hammer on anvil, the shouting of sailors, gales of drunken laughter and the shrieks of scolding women.

Wapping Wall had been built as an embankment against the tidal Thames on the eastern side of the triangle. The Commissioner of Sewers encouraged private building along the wall to help defray the cost of main-taining it and soon it was covered with warehouses, workshops and wharves.

There Ann Hooper kept a bawdy house (or so it was said) and, in the late summer of 1627, when Charles I had been king for two years, she fell out with some of her neighbours. There is no way of knowing whether it was an old feud, or a sudden explosion of the sort caused when a spark of irritation flies into the dry tinder of anxiety. Whichever it was, four law suits were started up, with suing and counter-suing among the locals.

It was an anxious time. The plague of 1625 had wiped out nearly 30,000 people in the metropolis, taking its highest toll in the insanitary suburbs and out-parishes. There were serious riots in Wapping and Ratcliffe in 1628 when the unpaid sailors from Duke of Buckingham's ill-equipped expedition to the Ile de Rhé were quartered there. The inhabitants hereabouts were more likely to be strangers than the inhabitants in the more prosperous parts and, mixed in with the country folk, were a good number of foreigners – Flemings, Swedes and Dutchmen in particular.

Ann Hooper sued Elizabeth Eaton and Elizabeth Willey; they both counter-sued and their husbands were drawn in, but this affair was clearly a petticoat brawl. And, what is more, they were all probably true whores.

It was a few weeks before Bartholomewtide, August 24. A group of women were standing about, chatting in a ships' carpenter's yard. There was a seaman's wife, a weaver's wife, several others and children at play. Old Goodwife Studde, whose husband's yard it was, started whipping one of the children. Ann Hooper, the brothel keeper, asked if the child's mother was an honest woman. The goodwife said that she was and Hooper replied: 'If the mother were an honest woman, the child cannot otherwise be an honest child'.

As reported, it seems to have been a mild enough remark, but probably Anne Hooper was reprimanding the goodwife for smacking the child. At all events, Elizabeth Eaton, one of the bystanders, who may well have been drunk, burst out laughing. Ann Hooper thought Eaton was laughing at what she had said and launched into abuse: 'Thou art a Tinker's Trull [moll], thou hast the Poxe in thy nose'.

Elizabeth Eaton, who may well have exhibited signs of pox, sued Hooper for those words.

Either on the same occasion, or at a similar gathering at Goodwife Studde's (the evidence in these cases is particularly confusing) Ann Hooper and her husband, John, got into argument with Elizabeth Willey. 'Thou has forgotten', said John in menacing tones, 'since I sett up a Badstead [bedstead] for thee, when as I felt thee and there was noe hair on thy private parts [another sign of the pox]. I . . . might then have been naught with thee or layan with thee'.

Ann Hooper chipped in: 'Thou hast a great belley, art with child, but it is none of thy husband's'.

Elizabeth Willey sued the Hoopers for those words.

Not long after, Elizabeth Eaton and Elizabeth Willey were caught standing outside the Hooper's house and shouting abuse in at the window.

'You whore', called out Eaton, 'was not a Flemminge fetched out of bed from thee or leapt from thee or leapt out of a window, when as you dwelleth at the next dore unto the Pope's Head in Wapping Wall?'

Willey followed with: 'You . . . lay with a Fleming for 2*s*. and an Englishman for half a crown. I would have used my own countryman better.'

If that was the going rate, when a labourer earned 1*s*. a day, these women could well afford the £5 or £6 needed to take their rivals to St Paul's for a public shaming.

The years leading to the Civil War

About a year after the Wapping bawds were at court, the High Church reformer, William Laud, was translated to the See of London and a moral and spiritual purge began. For five years he was Bishop of London and then, in October 1633, he became Archbishop of Canterbury and was in charge of the whole operation of quashing the Puritan sects, getting rid of Brownists, Anabaptists, along with Papists, atheists, fornicators, brawlers, and those who took their knitting to church. Woe betide whores, pimps, panders, rogues and rascals.

The Church was undoubtedly in a parlous state: ''Tis superstition, now a day', said the Archbishop, 'for any man to come with more reverence into a church, than a tinker and his bitch come into an alehouse'.

Thomas Swadlin, the new high churchman who had been appointed to Aldgate parish to deal with the disturbing Puritan element there, was speedily suspended for drinking in a local tavern while a substitute took a service in St Botolph's. That was a hint of what was to come for the citizens of London and, even more, for Ann Hooper, Elizabeth Willey, Elizabeth Eaton and all the others in the lawless suburbs.

In December 1634 the Commissary Court sat to look into the affairs of the diocese. Whole days were allotted to rough spots like the parishes of St Clement Danes and St Martin-in-the-Fields. Two weeks before Christmas, a contingent from Stepney came to the Long Chapel to be castigated and fined. About two hundred turned up, and another hundred had been summonsed. They were sailors' women and sailors, barmaids, bricklayers, labourers, carpenters, weavers, tailors, innkeepers; more women than men. The overwhelming majority of them were there because they had born, sired or delivered bastards. Matthew Grates, a Limehouse surgeon, turned informer and had a number of his clients up before the stern doctors from the Commons. Margaret Fuller from Wapping Wall was indicted for 'harbouring disorderly and incontinent persons'.

Back at Christchurch, Newgate, in the summer of 1636, now hung with so many paintings of saints 'that you would take the place for St Peter's in Rome', on the morning of the first day of June, Dr William Clarke heard an astonishing 158 office suits for the Archdeaconry between the hours of nine and eleven.

There were a group of parishioners from St Sepulchre who refused to pay their poor rate, and twenty-one (Puritans?) from St Andrew by the Wardrobe presented for not taking their Easter communion. A man from St Stephen Walbrook appeared to answer the charge that he had built a chimney which 'smokeath upon the church'. A barber from St Bennet, Sherehog had been trimming in time of divine service, and Thomas Keyes was indicted for putting his hands under Joane Fielde's coat in the vestry at St Andrew Undershaft.

The churchwardens at St Anne's, Gresham Street, were especially vigilant. They presented the inappropriately named Richard Wetnoll for keeping his hat on during the service and poor old Sarah Jones was brought before the judges because she had taken a dislike to the new pew the wardens had moved her to and kept going back to her old one.

Under the Laudian regime the Archdeacon's court was meeting almost daily, either in camera in the lawyers' chambers in Doctors' Commons, or in open court at Christchurch. There were more slander actions than usual. Women had reason to be genuinely fearful of the churchwardens, at this time. A presentment for immorality might not just lead to a small fine and excommunication. The Court of High Commission was fining people thousands of pounds and some were put in prison.

The activity in the spiritual courts was undoubtedly encouraging folk to take their enemies to task there in all manner of suits. The parishioners of St Brides, Fleet Street, got together to deal with a local trouble-maker by getting him to court for fathering a bastard. It was the keeper of the Poultry Compter who let the cat out of the bag by admitting he would spend £100 to keep the said Robert Finch in prison because he was 'so troublesome among his neighbours'. One of the witnesses, a timber dealer from the Bridewell, was so nervous of 'foreswearing himself' when he gave evidence that his hands shook. He claimed it 'was because he had the palsy'.

No wonder the cry went up 'Hunt Laud, the fox!'. How many sailors' girls were in the crowd on Tower Hill the chill January morning in 1645 when Archbishop Laud was executed? Was Ann Bolt who had been prosecuted for living with another man while her husband was at sea? Or Surling, the Ratcliffe trumpeter and his wife who had been fined for having a child before they married? Were the hard-working craftsmen there who had worked on holy days? Was old Sarah Jones from Gresham Street still around to give a cheer?

We will listen in on two affrays in the notorious Smithfield area, Ruffians' Hall they called it because of the duelling. It was the nearest large open space to the City and there had been an animal market there for many hundreds of years. The annual fair held there on St Bartholomew's Day was a riotous, debauched occasion. In the past the gallows had stood over by the horsepool. The dingy alleys and muddy lanes which led off it were some of the worst in London; one of them was Chick Lane, where Eleanor Meade lived, next door to John Sorrel.

One day near midsummer 1633 they had a squabble on their doorsteps, during the course of which he said he could prove her a whore: 'Thow wert brought home from Southwark in a porter's basket . . . a common and private whore . . . brought over London Bridge in a basket.'

The words were heard by the Derbyshire wife of the cutler next door, a porter's wife from the Isle Of Ely, a poulterer's servant from Northamptonshire, a Yorkshire-born barmaid, and a local scrivener.

Sorrel, realising, perhaps that he had gone too far this time, tried to smoothe things over. He went with his brother-in-law to Hallewell's victualling house, at the sign of the George at the top of Chick Lane 'over against the penns in Smithfield' where Eleanor Meade was drinking and discussing her intention to sue with the landlady. The two men entreated her to have a drink with them, at which she replied tartly: 'If she had a mind to drink she had 2*d*. in her purse . . . she could call for a can of beer as well as he'.

A wager of 6*d*. (or a quart of wine) was laid between Eleanor and John Sorrel as to whether or not Eleanor had said that Sorrell's wife was not worthy to wipe her shoes. The attempt to settle things failed; the lawyers were called in and charged a good deal more than 6*d*.

Meanwhile, Ralph Hubbersteade, the constable who lived in Long Lane, over the other side of Smithfield, was busy spreading malicious lies, or so it was claimed. A constable would not have been a popular figure in an area like this and Hubbersteade, from the sound of it, was a self-important bully who liked a good gossip. As he strode around the parish about his duty he was telling everyone that Ann Hoskins, who lodged with Bryan Nicholson and his wife, had: 'Taken a prick and that one Bryan had given it her'.

When Hubbersteade went into Richard Bruce's poultry shop in the market he asked Ned the carpenter if he had married Ann Hoskins yet. Ned said that she was 'boar'd already' and the constable informed him that it was Bryan's doing. Mistress Nicholson was in the shop: 'I marvell, Mr Hubbersteade', she said, with admirable restraint, 'that you being a master of a family and an officer in the parish, should use such words as to say my husband had begott Anne Hoskins with childe'.

Hubbersteade then told her to go back to her own stall, adding: 'Are there no more Bryans but one?'

A young apprentice told the lawyers that he was in his master's shop, in Long Lane, with Hubbersteade when Mistress Avery came in with Bryan Nicholson's wife: 'How now, Landlady', called Hubbersteade, 'What – has Nan Hoskins taken the prick and is she with child and has master Bryan fuck'd her and gotten her with child?'

Mistress Avery was not to be drawn, or so she said: 'How doe I know, you may as well doe it as he, for ought that I doe know!' While Mistress Nicholson, with dignity, told him he was 'fitter for a Shrove Tuesday boy than a constable', and Hubbersteade 'in a malicious manner', replied: 'Goe runn away with the butcher againe!'

Miseries of London (1807), by Thomas Rowlandson. Over a century and a half after Beaumont and Fletcher, London still had its Turnbull Streets. (The Guildhall Library, London)

The suit was brought by the Nicholsons, so it is unlikely to have been an attempt to get Ann Hoskins back in the marriage market. More probably it was cooked up by the Smithfield folk to put the bully Hubbersteade down.

Clerkenwell was thought by some to be worst area of all. Certainly Turnmill or Turnbull Street, which led up to Clerkenwell Green, had the reputation of being the roughest street in the capital. 'Here' wrote Beaumont and Fletcher, 'has been such a drinking, swearing and whoring . . . we have all lived in a continualle Turneball Street'.

On the other side of the Green ran St John Street and there, on a spring day in 1635 some children were playing. One of Mary Crookes's brood of four hit Frances Royden's daughter who rushed in to tell her mother. In no time Mistress Royden was at the Crookes's house, demanding to see the parents. The husband came to the door. 'You Roague, you Rascall, you copper nosed Roague! Cannot my children goe in quiett in the street for your bastards?', ranted Frances.

Mistress Crookes appeared in the doorway – one imagines her elbowing her dumb-struck husband out of the way: 'Who is this you call Roague, Rascall?', she demanded.

Frances replied: 'That Copper nosed Roague, your husband. Cannot my honest children goe in quiett for your bastards, you drunken queane? [You] have your bastards to the hospital – none of mine were in hospital!' ('Meaning thereby', adds the clerk who took the evidence, 'that the producent committed fornication or adultery with some other and that her children were unlawfully begotten.)'

Agnes Nash, an apple seller who was in the house, heard Mary Crookes's answer: 'I was never so drunke that ever I was brought home in a coach as you were!'

According to Anne Young who had come to 'fetch a pale of water', she said: 'I never pissed in a man's hatt and flung it out of the window as thou diddest'

Women will often come to blows over their children's squabbles and these two mothers were obviously a match for one another. The case of the scold of Wood Street, which came before the Archdeacon's court in the Trinity term of 1637, was a very different affair. Catherine Barnaby seems to have been a seriously deranged woman, who caused a great deal of trouble in the neighbourhood, ranting and suing, the sort who might easily have been branded as a witch under slightly different circumstances.

The parish of St Alban, Wood Street, was a more respectable part of town than Smithfield or Clerkenwell. There the Dickensons ran a girdler's shop just near where Catherine lived, and Mistress Dickenson, in particular, suffered a great deal of abuse from poor Catherine Barnaby. She had been ducked the previous years after the Dickensons had seen to it that she came before the justices at the sessions, and there was now a suit pending in Star Chamber. Catherine seems to have got some sort of petition up among the local tradesmen which they were now regretting and all turned up to court to hound her: a tallow chandler, a shoemaker, a joiner, a blacksmith and a weaver.

A deputation of them had gone to Catherine's husband, who lived apart from her, in a 'garden house' a mile or so away in Turnmill Street. He protested that the affair was nothing to do with him; he had tried to keep her from vexatious suits and had told her that she would 'never want' if she would live quietly with him.

Catherine made a daily nuisance of herself in the girdler's shop, and one of many attacks on the Dickensons is recounted: 'That drunken Queane hath murdered my child and smutherd it in a Rugg', she said of Mistress Dickenson. As for Mistress Dickenson's husband, he: 'Keepeth pretty wenches in his house and . . . hath coaches coming and going at his bake dore att all hours in the night and . . . hath such fidling and singeing and halloweing in his house she cannot sleep for it'.

Catherine then turned again on the wife: 'That drunken Queane that sitts here . . . hath made my husband spend £500 and hath now set him beyond the sea . . . she keepeth company with none but pedlars and Roagues'.

Catherine created continual scenes and, if anyone dared answer her back, it was said, she 'fetcheth a bottle of hay [bundle of hay] and setteth it up, and sayeth she cannot be Quiet for those roagues and Rascalles . . . she sets it up for them to scould at'.

Maybe Catherine's child had died, smothered in a rug. Perhaps it was that which unhinged her.

In Nell Gwynne's day

In the explosion of anger against the tyrant Charles I and his High Churchmen, the spiritual courts were abolished, along with the Monarchy and the House of Lords. For squabbling neighbours, Civil War provided ample opportunity for private revenge and, during the Commonwealth and Protectorate, justices of the peace and Cromwell's major-generals were vigilant for commotion; what slander suits there were went to the courts of common law.

With the return of the Monarchy the Church courts were restored. Not that the Doctors at the Commons had been idle, far from it. During the Interregnum the Archbishop's probate court, the Prerogative Court of Canterbury, had been 'nationalised' and, in the guise of a lay, state institution, dealt with probate matters for the whole country. In May 1660 they were ready to start the whole range of business again and re-establish themselves as the arbiters of morals in the capital.

But times had changed. There would be no attempt to reintroduce the repressive measures of the old Archbishop; no more mass purges and no High Commission to terrify folk into behaving themselves. Apart from bouts of attacks on Dissenters, the two bishops' courts and the archdeaconry withdrew from direct interference in moral affairs. But anyone who could afford it and had the inclination could still initiate suits.

Nell Gwynne, by Gerard Valck, after Sir Peter Lely. (National Portrait Gallery, London)

What with the new King and his brother leading the dance into sexual licence, Samuel Pepys close behind them, and Nell Gwynne with her 'lewd talk' performing at the King's House, one might think that the women of Smithfield and Wapping, taking their cue from their betters, would cease to worry about slights on their virtue. Not so. In 'good King Charles's golden days', the working women of London redoubled their efforts to take their neighbours to court for slanderous words.

It is difficult to understand why these bold Restoration women, who joined with their husbands and co-workers in the weavers' riots and were of Millamant's generation, were so anxious to have their reputations cleared. Churchwardens did not present as they used, and, even if they did, the punishment had lost its sting, especially if you were a Non-conformist, in which case banishment from the Church would be welcome.

The days were not so golden for the ordinary people of London, many of whom were Nonconformists and had supported Parliament. Now Church and Crown were back they were labelled 'conventiclers' and, in spite of the King's genuine attempts to introduce religious toleration, subject to bouts of vicious persecution. London was a tense, riotous place. When the apprentices rose in Cheapside in March 1664, in protest against two of their number being pilloried, Pepys heard the drums of the trained bands 'beating everywhere as if an enemy were upon them'. Memories of Laud's popish ways and suspicions about the King's undercover dealings with the Catholic Louis XIV created an exaggerated fear of Jesuits lurking in the shadows. There was rioting against papists, brothel burning and weavers' riots.

Only five years after the King's return, the worst plague ever known struck the city, followed by the Great Fire. Later came the harsh winters of the 1680s, when the Thames froze, fuel bills rocketed and many hundreds of watermen were out of work. There were new burdensome taxes: the hated Excise, the Hearth Tax and the crippling Poll Tax, much worse and more unpopular than its twentieth-century namesake. In 1681, the landlord of the Crowne alehouse in Long Acre had to pay 24s. a year chimney money, 6s. poor rate, 6s. to the dustmen, and 4s. each to the beadles for watch money.

The late seventeenth century was a boom time for brothels and bawds – Charles II himself was tempted to a bawdy house by the Earl of Rochester. The madam of a fashionable establishment said that, during the law terms, the London season, she would 'here of nothing less than half a Crown' and at other times 'a shilling would go down with her'.

Living conditions were harsh for the poor Londoner and there were plenty of warring whores around. A close look at the slander suits suggests that few of them were about good name. We will be listening in on cases which were clearly symptomatic of the mood of the time. Aggression born of the unresolved problems which the Restoration settlement brought exacerbated the tensions in overcrowded tenements.

This time we will see what is going on in the Consistory, the court where Charles Pepys and his wife took their matrimonial difficulties. Before the Civil War, that court had about the same amount of defamation business as the Commissary. After the Restoration, it had far more. Between Easter and Christmas, 1680, for instance, 117 cases were initiated, of which eighty-seven were slander and only one of them brought by a man sole. In perhaps 70 per cent of those slander cases the defendant was also a woman.

Again, it was from the poorer quarters that the squabbling neighbours came, no longer to St Paul's but to the new premises in Knightrider Street, rebuilt after the Great Fire. It is recognisably the same place which Dickens knew in the 1830s.

More records survive from this period and it is possible to get a clearer idea of what was going on. Enough sentences with costs are extant to show that suits cost about £5, at a time when servants' wages were £4 a year. We also know the outcome of most of these cases.

First we will go to Whitechapel, a mile outside the City's eastern gate, and observe some of the tensions which arose in a poor lodging house. Whitechapel had been well on the way to becoming a slum eighty years ago, when Stow deplored the 'pestering' of the wide high street with cottages for the meaner sort. It had its own theatre in Shakespeare's day, the Boar's Head, and its own prison. Most of the inhabitants either worked in the local gun-makers, iron and bell foundries, and the cloth trade, or were sailors. There was still enough open space, however, for Pepys to take a coach there to take the air.

The lodging house was in Black Lyon Yard, which backed on to Brick Lane. There lived Anne Shelley, who ran a victualling house, Margaret Ford and her husband, Jane Wilsen, an elderly, indigent widow, who had come to London forty years before, and, in a room beneath her, a Welsh farmer and his wife who had just arrived in the area.

One Friday in January 1681 Shelley and Sarah Jones, the farmer's wife, were visiting Mistress Wilsen, who was ill in bed. There were 'words of differ-ence' between the two women about a flannel cap which the invalid had mis-laid. Anne Shelley was annoyed with Sarah Jones for troubling the old woman, 'was sorry that she should come here, speaking to the said Mistres Wylson who then lay sick on her bed'. A slanging match ensued and Shelley said that Sarah was one of a 'pack' of whores and the other was Margaret Ford, who lived next door. She then 'started up and gave [Sarah Jones] a sound box on the ears'.

While all this was going on Sarah Jones's husband, Henry, came to the door of the room and looked in. He heard what was said and was not sur-prised, as Ford and Shelley had fallen out before. John Terrey, a tailor from Shoreditch, who was in the building overheard the shouts.

'Mistress Ford is a whore and a drunken whore, and God damn her, she would prove it', Shelley shrieked.

Sarah Jones ran out and into the Fords' rooms. 'Now that bitch . . . is gone to Ford's wife at the next door to tell her what I sayd of her. But she . . . is a whore, and a common whore . . . and 'tis known to all the parish,' said Shelley.

Margaret Ford laid her libel in the Consistory and the case was heard three months after the event. Anne Shelley had mustered some good support, including the Shoreditch beadle who said he knew all the householders in his parish and the tailor, Terrey, was not among them.

The invalid herself was bribed with 1s. to come to the Commons and denied that Mistress Ford had been discussed at all. Poor witnesses were normally paid 1s. by the party for whom they appeared; it was meant to be the equivalent of a day's wages, but had probably not kept pace with inflation.

Ann Atkins, a Yorkshire labourer's wife, came to assist in Ford's defence. The burden of her evidence was that Sarah Jones was such a disreputable character that her testimony should be discounted. Not only was she living in sin with Henry, her so-called husband, but she had previously lived, for sixteen years, with another to whom she was not married. A friend had asked the brazen creature whether she was not 'afraid of God to live in Adultery'; her reply was that she 'tooke this . . . [Henry] to better herselfe'.

But as far as the judges were concerned, Mistress Ford's lawyers had proved the slanderous words, and Ann Shelley was duly excommunicated and made to pay the costs.

Three suits emanated from a Fleet Street tenement in the same year. The White Horse inn seems to have been one of those towering half timbered edifices, with a gallery running round the inside, overlooking a courtyard. As the whole of the parish had been destroyed by the Great Fire, it must have been quite newly built.

The parish of St Bride's took in part of Fleet Street, a busy thoroughfare with a number of book shops. The Temple Bar end was the Trafalgar Square of the day, where 'pope' burnings and demonstrations tended to be held. The street had a reputation for lawlessness since Queen Elizabeth's time because of the number of large taverns near the bars: the Devil, the King's Head, the Cock and the Mitre were still there after the fire. The alleys leading off the street at the eastern end, where it sloped down to the filthy Fleet Ditch, full of dead dogs and garbage, were far worse. On the south side was the libertine area known as Alsatia, the haunt of thieves and prostitutes, and on the north side was the red light street par excellence, Fleet Lane. Pepys was afraid to meddle with the pretty wenches he saw lingering on their doorsteps, for fear 'they were not wholesome'. He went back again, 'God forgive me, out of an itch to look upon the sluts there', and when he saw them his 'stomach turned'.

There is no way of telling which part of the parish the White Horse inn was in, but one can guess.

All the plaintiffs won, so nobody achieved anything and all the parties suffered. The chief protagonists were two couples, a young coachman from Gloucestershire and his wife, called Richman/Richmond and another couple by the name of Holgate. One of the most active witnesses was Richman's nineteen-year-old apprentice from Dorset.

The Richmans sued the Holgates and the Holgates sued the Richmans, and the Richmans probably put their nursemaid up to suing the Holgates as well. It seems unlikely that any of the women were really much concerned about their 'dear, dear honour'.

The first suit was brought by Elizabeth Field, the Richmans' wet nurse, against William Holgate.

At the end of February or the beginning of March last, says the apprentice, he was cleaning his master's coach at the upper end of White Horse yard. He heard his master and William Holgate 'falling out' and, 'after they had been scolding a while', Elizabeth Field, who had been in the yard with them, went inside and Holgate called after her: 'You whore you. If I had knowne you had been goeing out of towne soe soone, I would have given you a whores' mark before you had gone!' The coachman, who was in his stable, said Holgate had called her 'that whore nurse'.

The young nurse also brought a separate action against Jane Holgate, who had accused her of selling her baby for pie meat: 'You whore, you Bitch! Where is your Bastard that you gave the skip kennell [footboy] a side of Pigg to get in Pye Corner.'

About a month after the affray over the nurse, there was a quarrel between Mistress Richman and William Holgate about a cockerel that was lost. This time Margaret Richman sued Holgate.

A Buckinghamshire coach-painter living in St Giles, recounts the tale. He, his wife and his journeyman were painting the Richman's coach in White Horse inn yard. He heard Holgate say to Margaret Richman: 'You Bitch, you whore, you were drunk and ledd up the yard between two foot boys by the Cunt, and I held the pott to thee whilst thou didst pisse in't'.

The apprentice, who was, again, out in the yard, says that the row started between his master and William Holgate, and Mistress Richman came out and joined in. He also says it was about a 'cock and a curry comb'. The judge decided his evidence was irrelevant, but nevertheless found for Margaret Richman and ordered Holgate to pay £6 costs.

The Holgates took revenge. Jane Holgate sued Margaret Richman for words spoken in April. One witness was the an ostler from the inn; he said that Jane Holgate was leaning over the rail of the gallery in the inn yard and Margaret, who was down below, called up: 'Thou art a whore and was knockd [up?] in the festry [barn] between two skuttles of oats'. A stage coachman's wife and a tailor's wife corroborated that evidence and added the words 'bitch, witch and jade' and 'boardie faced whore'.

The judges believed that, too, and Mistress Richman was excommunicated and ordered to pay the costs.

Of the witnesses in the White Horse inn case, at least four were either godless or conventiclers. William Holloway, the apprentice, said he only went 'last Sunday' to his parish church, St Brides, and before that to St Andrew, Holborn, for prayers and sermon and that he never received the sacrement. Richard Perrot, the coach-painter, said he 'never yet received the sacrement', and sometimes went to one church and sometimes another. His wife said she had not received the sacrament for two years. Another witness, a coachman, was evasive about his place of worship.

In the same term the lawyers were called in to apportion blame in yet another lodging-house feud. This one was in an area known for its houses of ill repute, Long Acre. Pepys's father-in-law lived there and when the coach set his wife down, the diarist was 'troubled to see her go thither . . . in so ill-looked a place, among all the bawdy houses'.

The lodging housekeeper was one Mistress Hills, a Scotswoman who liked her drink; most of the lodgers were fellow countrymen of hers. The house stood in Crown Court, one of the 'mazy courts and dark abodes' in the Drury Lane area. The suit was brought by two of the lodgers, a Scots woman and the man she lived with, Anderson. The defendant was the daughter of the owner of the house, a young woman called Elizabeth Bentley.

One June evening the lodgers were gathered in the housekeeper's room and a doctor's maid was complaining about her stepmother. Elizabeth Bentley, offering consolation, said: 'There was nowe good came out of that country!'

Mr Anderson, assuming, probably quite rightly, that the country referred to was his own, took offence. 'Who do you abuse?', he snapped.

Bentley said she was not speaking to him. 'You damn'd bitch', he went on, 'you did abuse a whole Nation for one!'

Bentley told him to go 'meddle with his own business', adding, for good measure, that he was a 'floundermouth dogg' and would be well advised to 'goe to his own wife in Scotland'.

She then turned on his companion: 'You whore and Queane . . . you Scots whore . . . you go like Man and Wife, but you live like whore and rogue'.

Fortunately Elizabeth Bentley's mother appeared at that point and hustled her daughter out of the room.

The scene changes to a 'little low room' in the Crowne alehouse, a vast drinking establishment nearby, with numerous bars. It is a few weeks later, the Andersons have laid their libel in the Consistory, and Bentley is there with her mother. The latter is tackling one Alice Westropp who has been engaged to give evidence against her daughter: 'God forgive you', expostulates Bentley, 'for I never spoke those words!'

Alice Westropp agrees to withdraw, but does, in fact, go to court. As she explained later, to the outraged mother: 'What would you have me doe? Master Anderson and his wife forced me to sweare, and called me a Thousand whores, and Threatened me that if I did not sweare against Mistress Bentley, they would ruin me.'

Master Anderson was determined to prove Bentley a brawler and had one of his witnesses repeat a conversation overheard in the same alehouse, in which Bentley's own husband had said she was a bitch. The defence argued that he had really been talking about a dog that had recently whelped in the court.

The trump card in Elizabeth Bentley's defence should have been the evidence given by an old friend of the housekeeper, Jane Cox, a widow from St Bartholomew's Lane. What she told the court made it clear that Anderson's woman was opposed to the whole business of suing and had been forced into it by her brutal lover.

Early one afternoon, not long after the affray, the old widow was visiting her friend at the lodging house. As she went in she encountered Mistress Anderson sitting on the stairs in floods of tears. Her 'husband' had been beating her for siding with Elizabeth Bentley. At that point Bentley appeared and Mistress Anderson, showing her injuries, sobbed: 'Bentley, I am obliged thus for takeing of thy part'.

'I am sorry for that', replied Elizabeth Bentley '—I am abus'd and must be undone, they say for taking of your part'.

Anderson's woman went on to explain that she had never intended to harm Bentley: 'The dogg [meaning Mr Anderson] can do nothing without aid, nor ever would. I answer in blood if it goe any further'.

The feeble Scot, it seems, enraged by Bentley's 'racist' remarks, had used this supposed slight on his mistress's good name to take his enemy to task before the Civilians. In spite of Jane Cox's evidence, he won his case, sentence of excommunication was passed on Elizabeth and she was ordered to pay costs.

When 'Dirty Doll' Winterbottom of Shoreditch sued Thomas Burton for words, it was almost certainly her 'man' who was behind it. A group of men were drinking together in the Winterbottom house in Shoreditch in January 1681, a woodmonger, two labourers and some others.

'Winterbottom, you keep three Cunts', said Burton, 'Mistress Pirce, Dirty Doll (meaning his then wife) and tother sits by you!'

The last of these cases demonstrates the influence which the bawdy Court at Whitehall had on the working folk of the capital.

Not far from the Scottish lodging house in Long Acre was a chandler's shop, at the sign of the Seven Stars. In that same summer of 1681 when Anderson the 'floundermouth dogg' fell out with his landlord's daughter, the shopkeeper at the Seven Stars, Jane Mitchell, was sued by one of her customers.

Chandlers' shops were not just places where soap and candles were bought; they supplied the staple breakfast of beer and bread and cheese for stallholders and others who could not afford alehouse prices. Oil, coal and cheese were also sold in small quantities to those who could only spare a couple of pence at a time.

Jane Mitchell and her husband, John, had crossed swords with their 'overthwart neighbour', Bessie Wells, over a 'reckening' and because she 'fetch'd her drink at another house'. They had taken her to the Marshalsea Court and won, buying a silver ink-horn with the profits of the exercise. It was time for Bessie to take her revenge. Stirred up by a 'tatling, tale bearing woman' who lived with her, Bessie took Jane Mitchell to the Commons for some words she had spoken in the shop one afternoon in August.

It was around the time 'when the King came from Windsor', said the witnesses, and the chandler's shop was full. A labourer's wife, a woman whose husband was a 'coachman to gentlemen', a founder's wife and a soldier were making their purchases and gossiping. The shopkeeper, as she weighed out the candles, announced to the assembled company:

> This Mistress Wells is a whore and a bawd, and I saw a coachman
> Grabble her up as high as the Elbowes. She is the Duke of Monmouth's
> whore and bawd, and gets her living by sheweing her Cunt. She lyes
> with all Nell Gwynne's footmen and I'll bring Nan Preston to prove it!

With that reminder of how the King led the way, we will leave the streets of London echoing to the sound of drunken scolds, falling out about 'bottle ale', flannel caps and curry-combs, only pausing to reflect that in these licentious times there was still the occasional soul who was afraid to God to live in adultery.

'Hatred pursued beyond the grave'. Searching in the Prerogative Will Office. From the *Pictorial Times*, 3 January 1846. (The Guildhall Library, London)

4

At the Court of Death

Families in will suits
at the Prerogative Court

THE SELF-STYLED 'NIGHT WALKER' on one of his evening rambles in search of lewd women met one in St James's Park who told him that she charged a guinea a night. When he protested she explained with a sigh: 'Why truly, Sir . . . I am a Gentlewoman by Birth, but my Father dying Intestate, a covetous, miserable Brother would not allow me any Portion'.

As the lady rustles off in her silks into the darkness of the royal park, we will leave the dim alleys and rough women who took their affrays to the bishops' and archdeacons' courts, and turn our attention to some of the more gently bred of the clients at the Commons. They have come, many of them, in mourning attire, about the most weighty problem of all, inherited money.

Our visits from the Commons this time will take us into country mansions and the elegant houses which faced on to the fashionable streets of post-Fire London, with the slums tucked behind their skirts. The knockers on the doors are muffled, indicating trouble within. Maids and nurses are moving quietly about curtained sick-rooms, heavy with the stench of death. There is some sobbing to be heard, but none of the passionate shrieks that echoed around the bedchamber in the Pepys family's tobacconist's shop in Lombard Street. It is the quieter, bleaker sound which speaks of loss.

We will go too with the black-plumed horses into churchyards overhung with yew, and thence to the proceedings in the best chamber, where crêpe clad family and friends sip Maderia, nibble on Naples' biscuit and wait to hear the lawyer read out the words on which their fate might depend: 'In the name of God, Amen. I, A, being of sound and disposing mind, make this my last Will and Testament . . .'.

There were many courts in the Commons for the proving of wills, but the most prestigious and the busiest was the Archbishop of Canterbury's Prerogative Court. In the old days before the Civil War, like the Consistory and the Commissary, it met in St Paul's and the fat registers, files and bundles of case papers, were kept in apple-pie order in the registry in Knightrider Street. After the fire its court sessions were conducted temporarily in Exeter House, in the Strand and then in the newly-built Common Hall in College Square. The Fire had destroyed many of the early records, though not the sacred wills themselves; the eighteenth-century antiquarian, William Furnivall, looked in vain through sack after sack for the list of Shakespeare's belongings

YOU are defired to accompany the Corps of the Reverend Mr. *John Poftlethwayt*, from his late Dwelling-houfe in S. *Paul's Church-yard*, to the Parifh-Church of S. *Auffin*, on *Wednefday* next, the 30th of *September*, 1713. at Four of the Clock in the Afternoon, by reafon there will be a Sermon.

Pray bring this Ticket with you.

Ticket for the funeral of an erstwhile inhabitant of St Paul's Churchyard, 1713. (The Guildhall Library, London)

which his executor must have submitted to the registry. His notes still survive in the archive: 'Searched for the inventory of Mr Shakespeare'.

For the most part, then, the records of those most acrimonious of legal battles, testamentary suits, were lost in 1666, so for our viewing of 'hatred pursued beyond the grave' we are largely confined to the later years of the court's existence, starting in those days when Nell Gwynne's footmen were the talk of Long Acre.

The clientele here is, by and large, very different from that which attended at the Archdeacon's Court or even the Bishop's Court, and the commissary of the Prerogative is a very important man indeed. In Cranmer's day it was not unusual for the Archbishop himself to preside in court. When the dowager Queen Henrietta Maria died in France in 1670 it was the judge of the Prerogative that Charles II sent to claim her jewels and treasures. To this court came the wealthy and titled, the heirs of the famous and successful, the grandest women and men in the land, countesses and royal dukes, even kings, to make good their claims to family fortunes.

To the registry in Knightrider Street came John Hall, Shakespeare's son-in-law to take probate of his father-in-law's will. Will Hewer, Samuel Pepys's old clerk, was here to have his employer's will proved and make sure he got the collection of model ships that had been left to him. Handel's servant brought his master's will to be registered, thereby ensuring that the fair copy of the manuscript of the Messiah went to the Foundling Hospital. Sir Joshua Reynolds and two others, executors of Dr Johnson, came with a document which bequeathed the residue of the estate to Johnson's black servant. Lord Nelson's executors came, after the Battle of Trafalgar, with the little red note book which contained the famous codicil to the Admiral's will. He left his mistress, Lady Hamilton, as a 'legacy to king and Country', that is to say, she was to be maintained by the grateful British people!

The age-old rule of *bona notabilia* specified that only those in possession of personal estate, cash, goods and leases, to the value of £5 in more than one diocese (£10 in London), were entitled to have their wills proved in the Prerogative. Those of smaller means had their lesser bequests checked by the officials of the archdeacon or the bishop or, if they had lived in a locality where there was a peculiar jurisdiction attached to an extinct monastery or a cathedral chapter, their last wishes were examined by a special tribunal.

In the early days of the Prerogative Court's existence, the fourteenth and fifteenth centuries, there were few whose estates qualified them for the Archbishop's attention. As the decades rolled by, inflation gradually reduced the value of £5. The entrepreneurial spirit which gripped early modern man meant that there was more movement from one diocese to another and an increase in investments in different parts of the country and abroad. The business of the Prerogative grew accordingly, particularly as it claimed jurisdiction over the personal estates of anyone who died overseas or had goods there. In 1810 the Bank of England ruled that henceforth they would only recognise a Prerogative probate. By the nineteenth century testators as humble as the writer's great-great-grandfather, a Bethnal Green milkman, had their wills taken to the registry in Knightrider Street.

The Court's main business was 'common form'. This meant, in the case of a will, that the document expressing the dead man's or woman's wishes was taken or sent to the registry, usually through an attorney, and checked through by one of the clerks there to see if it seemed to be an authentic document, and was witnessed and signed by the testator. If it seemed reasonable then the executor appointed in it, or the chief legatee, if the deceased had forgotten to appoint an executor, had to swear that they would abide by the terms of the will and would render an account to the Court. They had no need to go to London, the oath could be administered by their lawyer with a local clergyman or some other reputable body. A copy of the will with a small parchment grant of probate on it was then given or sent to the person who was responsible for carrying out its provisions. The original document was carefully filed away and a faithful transcript made on to sturdy vellum and bound up in a register so that anyone who cared to inspect it might do so, in the long search-room overlooking the gardens in Knightrider Street.

Even if the document was not in order, that did not necessarily prevent it being proved, if three people could be produced who were privy to its execution. It was a seemingly rather lax system which enabled even overheard death-bed utterances to be sanctioned as legal bequests without much difficulty. Before the law was changed in 1837 about a third of all wills were spoken or nuncupative.

Grants of administration were made in a similar way. If no will had been left, then the next of kin or widow applied to the court, stating their relationship to the dead person and making their claim. There were perhaps more opportunities for fraud in cases of intestacy, so the claimant had to get someone to enter into a bond with them, to the value of the estate, or double it, whereby they were obliged to distribute the assets according to law and answer to the Court.

Often no legal formalities were observed; there was no obligation to do so, and, as now, it was only if a large sum of money was involved or when some outside body, such as a bank or creditor, asked for proofs of ownership, that approaches were made to the Commons. In Dickens's *Pickwick Papers*, when Sam Weller's stepmother died, leaving her will scribbled on a piece of paper which she had put into the teapot on the mantelpiece, his father, Tony, was all for avoiding the lawyers and putting the will on the fire as 'It's all right and satisfactory to you and me as is the only parties interested'. Sam was horrified.

It was a system which relied on the sure rock of human self-interest and on common sense. By the seventeenth century, and before the introduction of death duties in 1796, as long as the fees were paid, the courts Christian had no interest in what happened to the money, unless children were involved, who might be left destitute to become a burden on the parish. By the third decade of the eighteenth century the courts even ceased to demand that an inventory of the deceased's goods should be made. It did not matter who benefited as long as no one objected. There was no occasion for close investigation of the claimant's relationship to the intestate or careful scrutiny of the shaky death-bed signature on the will. It would, in any case, have been impossibly difficult to check up on all the claims in that way, especially for the Prerogative which was dealing with clients from all over the country. The Civilians might rest assured, that if there was another 'wife' around who had a prior claim, a maidservant who had managed to extract a last minute will in her favour, or a distant relative who saw the estate slipping into the hands of the Treasury Solicitor for want of kin, then they would all be there, battering on the door at 6 Knightrider Street, ready to enter their caveat.

Fights in families tend to be fought with greater venom than is to be found in altercations between strangers. Just before Christmas 1664 Samuel Pepys went to the Commons in the matter of the estate of his brother, Tom.

There were, he says 'A great many and some high words on both sides'. In probate litigation, perhaps even more than in matrimonial causes, the deepest desires and needs of the human heart are touched. Who does not crave the love and approval of their parents? Who would not fight to the death to have that love expressed in the form of a legacy which, into the bargain, would ensure material security? A will might rescue a beneficiary from the shame of living on the parish or in a debtor's prison, from the necessity of making a financially advantageous marriage or even from following the career of the lady in St James's Park.

There were rich pickings at the Commons for the proctors and advocates, as Dickens observed, not least from the exploitation of sibling rivalry. Like jackals tearing a corpse apart, brothers and sisters took issue over their fathers' estates, remembering and highlighting the magnified insults of childhood. The court provided a splendid battleground with rules and rewards for all manner of family antagonisms.

As we have noticed in other parts of the Commons, there are many women around. Although you will not find many female wills in the registers in those days before the passing of the Married Women's Property Act (1882) by the Restoration period it was the norm for married men to appoint their wives as executrixes and women comprised a good half of the litigants. Black petticoats swish through the stately courtyards south of St Paul's as widows join battle with their mothers-in-law over all that is left to show where their dead husband or son's preferences ultimately lay – his money. The wicked stepmother lurks here, determined to take Cinderella's entitlement for her own children. With them are the nurse-keepers and maids who witnessed the death throes and final utterances and are able to give an informed opinion about whom the dead man loved most.

Among the high and mighty litigants, there are some of the rougher sort. The Prerogative's jurisdiction lay over those who died out of the country and that included sailors who died at sea. The French wars in the eighteenth century brought in a good deal of custom. The naval landlady was a common feature in testamentary suits. Many a lad left everything to some kindly woman who had, perhaps, taken the place of his mother, or so the Court was persuaded.

There are a good number of representatives from the medical profession around, apothecaries who prescribed for the dying, and surgeons and physicians who attended them, all of whom are in a strong position to give an opinion as to whether the dying man was of a 'sound and disposing mind'. Scriveners might be seen scuttling about with their pens and papers; they are here to assess the signatures of testators and witnesses. Another noticeable group are, rather unexpectedly, those associated with the licensed victuallers' trade, landlords of taverns and alehouses, tapsters, barmaids and potmen.

Testamentary lawyers are very interested in alcohol. The crucial issue in many of the disputes here is the state of mind of the testator. As we have noticed, in the company of the scolds, it was a heavy drinking society and high alcoholic consumption was by no means confined to the lower orders. A very usual argument proffered by those disputing a will was that the testator was too drunk to know what he was doing when he made it. Many probably were. Quite apart from the habitual drinker who had a few too many and in a fit of boozy camaraderie left his estate to his mates in the alehouse, brandy and other alcoholic concoctions were used as pain-killers. Before the present century people did not usually make wills until they were 'pinched with the messengers of death', so the likelihood of their being incapacitated by drink or drugs when they made their final disposition was greater than it is now.

Doctors and madhouse-keepers were often called to the Commons to address the question of the mental capacity of some party deceased. The proctors themselves said that the most serious contentious business they handled concerned the competency of testators. Insanity was so commonly alleged in testamentary suits that when old William Hayward, the maltster of Truddox Hill in Somerset, approached death, he refused to make a will on the grounds that if he did someone would try and prove that he was mad. All his hard-earned money would, moreover, be spent on lawyer's fees. Sadly, the people with whom he lodged produced a piece of torn paper which they said was his will, and in the litigation which ensued 50 per cent of the £300 which he had left was spent in exactly the way he had feared. Half the village trudged into Frome to give their evidence to the mini-court which sat in session in the George Inn.

It was left to the Civilians to make the fine distinction between lunacy and eccentricity. Some claims were very borderline. Humphrey Bawden took up with the Quakers, much to his wife's disgust, and left a will benefiting the poor of that sect. When he died his family tried to get the will overturned on the grounds of his insanity; the chief burden of their proof was that he shaved his legs. When James Pilgrim Warner died in Newington, Surrey, in 1801, the family said that his behaviour rendered his bequests invalid:

> He frequently painted or blackened his face . . . would hang out his linen
> to air when the weather was damp, water the garden when it rained,
> pump his hat full of water and put in on his head and wet his breeches
> and afterwards wear them in that condition.

The ranting and hallucinations associated so often with death throes were often evinced as sure proof that the dying man was not in a fit state to dispose of his assets. The Earl of Anglesey died in 1702 and his brother and heir-at-law told the court the Earl had said 'the Devil was a dead rat' and claimed to keep the 'moon in his closet'.

The most difficult task for the judges must have been the decisions which had to be made about the judgement of a man or woman who was suffering from 'melancholy' or clinical depression. Among the evidence taken by the examiners at the Prerogative is enough material to disabuse those who imagine depression and work-related stress are modern fancies. The witnesses who came to court when two female relatives of a herald joined battle over his estate were asked: 'Was he not melancholy and of a reserved temper?' The interrogatory went on:

> Do you not know or have heard that such indisposition of mind proceeded from the Deceased's believing he had made some mistake in drawing up a Grant of arms and that he was much terrified and affrighted least he should be accused of forgery for so doing?

The poor chap's paranoia had got the better of him and on the night of 2 May 1720 he stabbed himself eighteen times.

The sort of evidence given in the probate actions in the Commons were very different from what was produced in the King's Courts because of the state of the law. The courts spiritual had no say over three most important aspects of inheritance. The Church had long been banished from having any say in the disposition of real property, freehold and copyhold land, although leases came under their purview. Disputes over property were dealt with by Chancery or King's Bench. In addition, it was not supposed to deal with matters arising from the contents of wills. Questions of what construction might be put on a testator's words, or whether a trust was legal, would be dealt with in the Chancery. Furthermore, by the seventeenth century, nobody went to the courts Christian in a straightforward attempt to get hold of a legacy which had been withheld, although there was a preliminary action 'in inventory and account'. Thereby the frustrated legatee or creditor of the estate could at least get the executor to reveal what assets there were and what he had done with them.

The suits, as far as wills were concerned, concentrated on the authenticity of the document itself and on the soundness of mind and emotional attachments of the man who made it. Most intestacy cases were 'interest causes', wherein parties contended to prove that theirs was the closer relationship to the deceased and that they were, thereby, entitled to administer the estate and get a share of it. There were strict regulations governing that, enforced by statute, but the Civilians ran an equitable ship and, if it was a case of deciding between the entitlement of a neglectful son and a devoted daughter, the latter had a good chance of success.

The witnesses who came to court in probate actions were there mainly to describe in close detail exactly what happened when the will was made; how Nell Gwynne, gasping for breath, was propped up on pillows by her maid while her chaplain hastily scribbled down her final wishes on the back of a letter from his sister, leaning on a japanned trunk to do so.

No part of the dying process was considered too intimate or grim to be brought up if it might have some bearing on who was to benefit financially. Sir Thomas Woolrych's estate was considerable and his will a document of vital importance, as he himself realised. When the dispute came to court his clerk gave his account of what happened just before Christmas 1661. He was in his employer's chambers in Gray's Inn, lighting the fire, when he was summoned to Woolrych's lodgings, where he found the old man sitting in a chair in his bedroom. Sir Solomon Swale was in the room and produced 'a writing on four or five sheets' which he offered to Woolrych, telling him it was his (Woolrych's) will. The sick man took it and kept it firmly in his hand 'Untill he had a desire to go to the stoole, and being helped to the stoole . . . he . . . was to put down his breeches'. One of the women helping him took the will and put it under the pillow of his bed.

No aspect of the deceased's behaviour was safe from the investigations of the lawyers if it might indicate something significant about his or her state of mind. Mad Mrs Morice caused a flurry in Southwark a few years before Victoria came to the throne, by leaving seventeen wills and a great deal of money. One prim spinster in her thirties, called to the Commons to add her bit to the mountains of evidence that accumulated in this most expensive of suits, was so embarrassed when she had to explain how Mrs Morice went to the lavatory, that she was unable to spell it out to the examiner and wrote it down herself in the book of depositions.

It was an important part of the witnesses' task to draw back the curtain on family feelings, to repeat the nasty remarks made by one member about the other, to catch the nuances of resentment, dislike and bitterness and to convey the expressions of 'affection dying the power of death'. Here was an exposée nearly as uncomfortable as any inflicted by today's press. No wonder Maria Lumsden, when she dictated her last wishes in 1661, added the heart-felt plea: 'And for God's sake let there be no falling out about it!' What range of emotions must have shivered through the litigants as they sat with their supporters in the Common Hall and listened to the grand Doctors of Civil Law tossing around their own loves and hates on the horseshoe platform? The proctors, sat below them, poring over the damning accounts of bribed servants and disappointed lovers. The one saving grace was that there was no live cross-examination and Miss Daniel of Southwark was not forced to blush and stammer in the witness box as she explained that Mrs Morice pissed with her maid. The Cinderella of Wapping, who we shall hear more of in due course, did not have to stand up before her wicked stepmother in full court and recount the cruelties she had sustained. And, after all was said and done, for those who won, there were rich rewards.

It might be argued that there was more at stake in the 'court of death' than in the 'court of scolds' or even in the matrimonial actions. The 'prize money' might be a large fortune, and even though the Prerogative had no direct say in what happened to the landed estates, there is no doubt that the decisions of the Civilians as to the validity of a will and the identification of the true wife or next of kin affected what subsequently happened in the equity or common law courts in the next round of the fight. Failure to secure even a small legacy, on the other hand, was, for some, the beginning of the end, a step towards a pauper's grave. Some women and men were prepared to

Top: *The Reading of the Will*, by W H Lizars. (National Gallery of Scotland, Edinburgh.)
Bottom: *The Reading of the Will Concluded*, by Edward Bird. (Bristol Museums and Art Gallery.)
From cottage to drawing-room the contents of the will evoke the same range of emotions from hatred to joy

take great risks in the desperate game and part of that risk was the blackmailing, suborning and bribing of witnesses. In some cases a very motley crew of dubious characters turned up to lie for a share in the profits. The judge in *Streete v Streete* (1668) proclaimed:

> Noe further credit [is] . . . to be given to the pretended sayings and depositions of Tristram Clement, John Bushell, Robert Spring [and seven more named] . . . They were and are varying, vacillant, single, contrary and repugnant to each other in theie sayings . . . intimate friends of the party producing them, but Capitall enemies of the party against whom they are produced, poore, needy and of ill life and conversation, such as have bin taught how and what to depose.

The thoroughness of the proctors is well exemplified in probate actions. If twenty-eight affidavits were called for in Dickens's fictional vestry brawl, how many more were needed to support the weighty financial causes in the Prerogative? What the author called the 'sundry immense books of evidence' are the enormous tomes which bind up the page upon page of examinations in chief and answers to interrogatories which survive to tell the tale.

The professionalism of the bar and bench which serviced the Prerogative and its prestigious reputation attracted contentious business from courts all over the country. Many a will came to Knightrider Street to be fought over after a probate grant had been made on it elsewhere. The rule of *bona notabilia* counted for less and less as the years passed and local attorneys increasingly took their contested business to firms of proctors like Dickens's Spenlow and Jorkins in *David Copperfield*.

Through the sunlight and shadows which patchworked the paved courts of Doctors' Commons walked the clients of the Prerogative, heavy with 'hatred pursued beyond the grave'. There were angry widows, like Margaret Weller who had kept her husband locked up for three years so that he grew an immense beard, punishment for preferring her sister. Jealous mothers-in-law, greedy neglectful sons, beleaguered stepchildren, bitter poor relations met with spiteful servants and profligate earls. The devilish wind which howled around Dean's Court blew the longest when the Prerogative was in session.

Cinderella

Let us meet some children and, appropriately in their company, some figures from nursery tales. The wicked stepmother, selfish ugly sisters, the younger son 'cut off with a shilling', the poor widow, the rich uncle, the miser, the babes in the wood are familiar characters from the old stories and all of them, real as you or I, appear in the evidences which came before the probate judges. Cinderella appears more regularly than most.

Before she is brought out from her kitchen, we will take a look at the part children played in affairs at the Prerogative. They were not often to be

A sentimental Cinderella. From *Cinderella and the Glass Slipper* (1854), illustrated by George Cruikshank

seen in the Commons, but slipped in among the black cloaks you may catch the occasional glimpse of small figures, also in black, some of them quite young. The Civil Law in its modern-seeming wisdom recognised the rights of children to choose who should be responsible for them. As soon as they reached their seventh birthday they could, as little George Carteret did in 1675, aged seven-and-a-half, elect their own 'curator' or guardian. He chose his grandfather to look after his affairs, now that his father was dead. His quite grown-up signature on the power of attorney or 'curation proxy' has survived to remind us that there were a number of weak and helpless human beings at the mercy of the pomp and circumstance of the Prerogative.

The number of curation proxies registered in the huge volumes known as Acts of Court Books bear witness to the importance of children in probate matters. When John Godolphin wrote his work on testamentary law in 1701 he called it *The Orphans' Legacy*. The likelihood of a child losing one, or even both, of his parents was much greater in past centuries than it is today and the provision of support for orphans and stepchildren was something which might be dealt with by all members of the legal profession. The City of London had its Court of Orphans where those responsible for the estates of minors had to submit an inventory or run the risk of being imprisoned. The Lord Chancellor took over the custodial duties of the Court of Wards in 1662.

The Prerogative and the other probate courts were responsible for making sure that the interests of the stepchild and the orphan in their parents' personal estate were cared for, and that legacies left to them were kept secure until they reached their majority. Fathers might appoint their under-age children as executors' though a suitable *administrator durante minori aetate* had to be appointed to look after the personal estate until the children could do it themselves. Anyone with the child's interests at heart could go to the court and get an inventory exhibited to ensure that the assets were not being eaten up. Wills which benefited the children of the testator were accounted 'privileged', and those who promoted them had a good chance of winning in a suit. It was, according to the lawyer Blackstone, a 'groundless, vulgar error' that fathers could cut a child off with a shilling. Some tried, like John Jacob Vesenbeck, a German seal-maker, who died in 1730. One son was thus dismissed 'for his extreme wickedness to mee'. The other was provided for, as Vesenbeck feared that his wife, who was inhumanly cruel to the boy, would starve him, so that he would 'schüt so small as a mouse'. This will stood but might have been overthrown as being 'deficient in natural duty'.

In cases of intestacy the courts' role was even more vital and it had been the ancient practice to take the distribution of such estates into their own hands when minors were involved. During the Interregnum some widows were obliged to enter into 'portion bonds' to make sure that their children or stepchildren got what was owing to them from their dead father, uncle or grandfather. Sir Leoline Jenkins, who was appointed Judge of the Prerogative in 1668, tried to revive the obsolete practice of distribution or limitation, as it was called in some of the other courts:

> Great mischiefs do daily occur since this ancient course has met
> with interruption. For instance, a man dies without a will and leaves
> ten children . . . if the eldest or any of them do get administration
> by himself, the other nine . . . will have no share in their father's
> estate.

The situation was exacerbated by the Common Law which favoured primogeniture: 'The eldest brother must have all, and all the rest that which the cat left on the malt heap'.

There was too much opposition from the common lawyers to permit a revival of the Church's intervention, but new legislation, the Statute of Distributions (1670), did at least put children's entitlement to their share in the money on a legal footing. Furthermore, 'strict settlement' was on the increase: following a solemn conclave, a document would be executed whereby the head of the family conveyed his real property in trust, taking a life interest for himself and his wife and entailing it on the eldest son or child of the marriage, and making provision for other members of the family, including jointures for the girls. Had the father of the prostitute of St James's Park done that, she would never have met the 'Night Walker'.

The care of children was, then, at the root of much of what went on in the Commons, and their representatives, often grandparents, of both sexes, were busy there about their charges' affairs. Minors rarely appeared themselves, except, perhaps, to go into the office of Spenlow and Jorkins, holding tight on to a grown-up hand, to practice their newly acquired writing skills by putting their name on the guardianship document. Occasionally, when no adult witness was available, they might have to take a more active part. One little girl did in the year of the Great Plague, and it is worth listening to what she said, to get a very rare hint of how a seventeenth-century eleven-year-old saw the strange and fearful world around her.

A wealthy man called John Baker died in 1664. His niece-in-law, Mary, was fond of him and a regular Sunday afternoon visitor to his lodgings in Clements Lane after she had been to church. On one of those visits, he had told her that he had 'cutt off' his heir-at-law, a cousin called Hibbins, and that he intended to leave his money to Mary and her children. As has been seen, the state of the law was such then, that spoken wills were quite acceptable if there were enough witnesses. In this case the only witness, apart from the beneficiary, was Mary's eleven-year-old daughter, Elizabeth.

Under normal circumstances, one suspects, there would not have been much chance of this 'will' standing up in court, but John Baker had, apparently, named Sir Anthony Bateman, Knight and Lord Mayor of London, as his executor. So, with some pushing from a relative called Day, who was a linen draper in Cheapside, Mary went to the Commons with her daughter. They took the oath in court and, a few days later were ushered in to the chambers of Sir William Meyrick himself, the Commissary and Chief Judge. The relevant documents were read to the child and she was asked a number of leading questions. The clerk wrote down her replies:

> To all the articles of the allegation and to the will nuncupative . . . being read unto her and the meaning of them declared unto her, she sayd that she understood not the words, articles or allegation, but by the word 'will' she conceived that to be a telling who shall have a man's goods when he is dead. And she saith that on a Sunday in an afternoone hapning about four or five Sundays before the death of Mr John Baker, who lived then neare St Clement's church, without Temple Bar, [she went] with her mother, Mary Baker, with the said Mr Baker in his chamber within the house of one Mistress Wood and at that time she heard the said Mr Baker tell her mother that Sir Anthony Bateman was his executor. She said that an executor was one who was to order a dead man's goods.

> [She] has known her age from tyme to tyme these two or three years last past. [She] hath heard and believes that she was christened at Cranham,

Gloucestershire [her godparents are named] and she shalbe twelve years of age if shee live till Michaelmas next.

. . . Till Christmas she went to schole among children but she hath not been at schole ever since Christmas last past.

[She has lived with her mother and is] subject to her correction when she displeaseth, but the last tyme her said mother did correct her or whipp her she remembreth not.

She knoweth that an oath is given by the Judge to a person to speke the truth and if any person shall not, upon oath, speak the truth, they are false persons and not to be trusted, but what punishment is due to any person swearing falsely she knoweth not, but now hath been told [did Sir William Meyricke lean forward and explain at that moment?] that God would not blesse her but punish her heare and hereafter if she should forswear herself and, for that reason she will speake nothing but the truth.

By her mother's commission [she] wayted on her to Doctors' Commons as ['they call' crossed out] the place is called and was here in a place where was a great company and one man sitting alone above all whom her mother told her was a Judge. And when she was there some person . . . told her she must kiss the bible and sweare upon it to speake the truth.

Her mother nor any other did tell her that she should have a hundred pounds to her portion or any other sums of money or a new coat or sugar plumes or gloves or any other thing if she would swear in this cause for Sir Anthony Bateman.

[She did not want to swear on the Bible] at last, not her mother, but somebody else there, told her that the judge would excommunicate her if she would not swear, and for fear of being excommunicated (which she had heard was a very strange thing) she was . . . contented to swear.

[It was not her mother but her cousin Day who] gott her to come unto this place where the Judge was . . . her mother was unwilling to have her come unto the place . . . she was not taken by her mother to be beaten if she would not come.'

When threatened with excommunication by someone (who, she refused to say), the child 'cryed for fear hereof'.

One can only hope that poor little Elizabeth Baker's ordeal was worthwhile and she got her new coat or at least some sugar plums. As the terrified eleven-year-old gazes around her in the dark panelled court room we will slip out and walk down to St Paul's Wharf, where a waterman may have a boat to take us down river to Wapping in search of Cinderella.

Before the twentieth century couples rarely lived together as long as they do now. The early death of a mother or father did regularly for children what divorce now does and provided them with step-parents. Second and even third marriages were as common as they are today. According to psychologists, the task of replacing a dead mother or father, who is enshrined forever in the golden haze of a child's longing, loving memory, is more difficult than taking over from one who has left home. Accounts of wicked stepmothers occur often enough, in fiction and in reality. In the thorough investigations conducted by the courts Christian, there is more chance of getting at least a clue as to what the stepmother had to contend with than can be found in a fairy tale.

In the late seventeenth century Wapping has grown a good deal since Goodwife Studde and the other brawlers at the 'court of scolds' were abusing one another all those years ago. There are more sailors and ships' repair yards and probably more brothels than there were then. As the English navy has grown in importance, so has Wapping, and many of the successful seafaring men have had houses built here.

In 1699 a suit was brought in the Prerogative by the daughter of a Wappinger called Roger Faucus. Like most of his neighbours, he was a seafaring man who, as master and part-owner of the ship *Adventurer*, had a contract from the Ordnance Office to take horses and other supplies to the Army in Ireland. On one such expedition, about ten years earlier, perhaps supplying horse for 'King Billy' to fight the battle of the Boyne, he had died, leaving Margaret, a teenager, in the care of his second wife, Jane.

Jane had three children of her own and a widow's life was not easy. Margaret suffered cruel punishments at her stepmother's hand and after ten long and miserable years, now safely married to Prince Charming, she took her revenge. Having carefully marshalled her evidence and recruited support from friends and her father's old acquaintances, she began a suit in inventory and account, which brought accusations of fraud against Jane Faucus, since remarried to a man called Clarke. The owners of the *Adventurer* were among her supporters, for they already had a bill in Chancery against Mistress Faucus for £1,400 which she owed them.

The widow was accused of falsifying the inventory of her husband's assets. His share of the profits of the Irish expedition had been £435 and she had declared only £57 8s. 9¼d. The submission of such a precise amount, calculated down to the last farthing, might have aroused suspicions before. She had charged the estate £18 for 'meat, drink, washing and lodging' of her stepdaughter for a year and two months, when the girl had only been with her for eight or nine months. She concealed £150 owed to the deceased from Sir Peter Rich's executrix.

The court, moreover, heard a sorry tale of Jane's treatment of Margaret. Bridget Swan, the widow of one of Margaret's father's old shipmates, said that at the time of Faucus's death Margaret was apprenticed to her and when her 'time expired' she went back to live with her stepmother. She was made to sleep on the floor in the pigeon loft over the wash-house in the yard. Hannah Corne, who lived in Milk Alley, near Wapping Old Stairs, said that Margaret was in 'soe very meane a condition that noe body cared to entertain her'. There were holes in the roof of the pigeon loft and 'the snow beate or drove into the room'. Margaret herself said:

> [she] was treated with such Barbarity and Cruelty by her said mother-in-law who would not permitt or suffer her to lodge and lye in the House but turn'd her into an Outhouse or Dovehouse being open to the Air and weather And without windows or shutts.

She was forced to eat with the servants and to look after the younger children and her stepmother would continually 'find fault with her shifts' and beat her for it. Fortune Mann, a young sailor from Durham (the 'Buttons' of this Cinderella story), had been shown her scars and related that Mistress Faucus did 'upon slight or no occasion . . . with a knife cutt and mangle her upon her Face, Head and Arms. And sometimes with the Tongs or anything els which came next to her Hands beat and bruize her'. Margaret told Fortune that 'she should carry her markes that shee had given her to her grave'.

The neighbours were all aware of what was going on and eventually Margaret 'was forced to go from her and shift for herself'. Hannah Corne took her into her house in Milk Alley. She spent some time in Newcastle, perhaps with some lad she had taken up with from the colliers' boats which came daily to Wapping Dock.

A battered Cinderella? Detail from one of George Cruikshank's illustrations to Henry Fielding's *Joseph Andrews*, from *Roscoe's Novelist's Library* (1831–1833)

Jane Faucus's defence was that her stepdaughter was dirty, disturbed and impossible to handle. She used 'saucy language', was 'of a very turbulent spirit and did behave and carry herself very undutifully and disrespectfully to her stepmother . . . and by her ill and savory language very much provoked her'. The bedroom she had been given was 'very warm and convenient'; her own children often slept there. This statement rather conflicts with what she went on to say. The girl:

> Did ly upon a good bed . . . [and] would very often foul and bepisse the Room and bed whereon she lay and was so very nasty that it was not proper or convenient to let her ly in a good Roome or bed.

Cinderella's wicked stepmother might have said just that, had she been given the opportunity. There was probably some truth in what was claimed by both parties, but our sympathies cannot help but lie, like the sympathies of the society which shaped the fairy tale, with the lonely girl in the chilly pigeon loft, not with the harassed widow overburdened with debts. Charles Dickens would have been surprised to know that the self-satisfied, port-drinking Civilian lawyers had ever played the role of fairy godmother in that 'very pleasant profitable affair of private theatricals'.

Thirty years later in a Cornish farmhouse Johanne Bewes was suffering at the hands of two stepmothers. George Warmington, of St Stephens near Launceston, died intestate in 1727, leaving three grandchildren, Mary, Johanne and George and an estate which included land worth £4,000 a year. Their father, Degory Bewes, took administration. Ten years later Mary was dead, George was still a minor, and Johanne was married to one Gautier. The children had never received their share of the grandfather's estate; their father had hung on to the assets, using some of it to educate children by his second marriage. The Gautiers started inventory and account proceedings against him in the Prerogative, and the letters which were exchanged with the local attorney and the lawyers at the Commons survive.

Gautier told the proctor acting for them that Degory Bewes was untrustworthy, crotchety and obstinate and that he had been 'cajoled into a third marriage' by a young widow with two children. The new wife had taken over the running of their affairs when Degory became senile. What is more, said Johanne Gautier:

> Mr Bewes keeps from us our late mother's marriage settlements, by which we are told we are entitled to her fortune; and 'tis to be feared he will be prevailed upon to destroy the writing . . . New settlements will be made on this woman and her children to the ruin of our brother George . . . and the destruction of our family.

Quite apart from all that, Johanne Gautier née Bewes, had been 'Under her two last mothers-in-law . . . put to the drudgery of a servant maid', and her husband reckons, that, if nothing else, she should be reimbursed for the housework she was forced to do for her wicked stepmothers.

Old Bewes, or his wily young wife, finally produced an inventory of the grandfather's goods which was delivered to the attorney in Launceston. When it was shown to the Gautiers, Johanne said that it was 'Very insufficient and Evasive and is sorry her father should be so faulty when he is on his oath'. When her grandfather died they had found a large canvas bag in his trunk, full of gold and silver coins; she remembers her father making a snide remark at the time: 'He wondered how Mr Warmington could plead poverty when he had so much money by him'. There is no mention of the bag of coins in the inventory, or of his silver tankard, brass candlesticks, his pewter dishes and all manner of other valuable household items.

Degory Bewes was said to have no regard at all for the powers of Doctors' Commons and the case went to Equity, as was increasingly the trend in the eighteenth century. The Church courts had no real powers to call in the assets, and actions in inventory and account finally ceased altogether. From the middle of the eighteenth century the Cinderellas would have to seek their revenge in the monstrous, long-winded operations of the Court of Chancery.

The cruel stepfather puts in far fewer appearances in stories than his female counterpart. Mothers are usually closer to their children and so the demon which bedevils a child's imagination is more likely to be her replacement that the remoter stepfather. The absence of the wicked stepfather from the Commons suggests that he had less opportunity than the second wife did to appropriate his stepchildren's rightful inheritance.

Natural fathers might be apprehensive about how their widows would behave towards children of a previous marriage, but they were very much more concerned to protect their offspring against the grasping wiles of any man which their widow might take up with after their demise. Even more, they were anxious that their own children's inheritance should not be stolen by subsequent stranger children which their widow might bear. Various legal contrivances, evolved to meet those needs, were indicated in wills and marriage settlements. In many cases, a widow sacrificed what her first husband had left her if she remarried.

What happened in the matter of the estate of Tobias Wyseman of Plymouth shows what lengths a man had to go to get hold of money which belonged to his wife's children.

Tobias Wyseman died in the year 1669 leaving two little boys, one named after him and one called William. His widow, Elizabeth, called Bett, was expecting another child at the time of Tobias's death, but was, nevertheless soon married again to a fortune hunter called John Johnson.

Leaving his pregnant wife at home Johnson rode off to London on a secret mission. The next we hear of him is that he is at Doctors' Commons, having procured a 'strange woman' to 'personate the said Elizabeth'. The couple went to the probate registry at 6 Knightrider Street and got a grant of administration made to them in the goods of Tobias Wyseman deceased.

As we have seen, the making of a grant was a straightforward affair, with no proofs of identity required. All Johnson had to do was produce some securities and take an oath. The plan was successful so far, but Elizabeth found out what was afoot through some friends in London and was, understandably, very upset and angry. A suit ensued, conducted by her mother, Elizabeth being about to give birth any day and in no fit state to do itself. Household servants and the Wyseman's legal friends were examined before the Mayor of Plymouth to confirm the women's story. When Johnson saw the instrument of renunciation in his mother-in-law's favour, he was thrown into a panic and, like Stoney Bowes, threatened his wife one minute and tried to cajole her the next. Johnson wrote to Elizabeth:

My dear honest and faithful wife,

It was my happiness this day to see your hand and seal against yourself; that you will find, I will assure you! But however, I value it not, for there is no person able to frustrate me of the same, for the Judge has decreed the same to me and I am now become Administrator.

But wife, I thought that you would never assign your hand and seal against your husband, for I see you have more love for your mother than you have for mee. You must expect that your mother cannot live for ever. Pray confide in your mother, if you please, but, I will assure you, I shall have something to say to your mother very speedily. Your mother will be turned out of a great deal of money before shee is aware of it – say that I say soe, for you must expect that London is able to give a man better advice of Law than Eastlick, and that assure thyself. Thy mother – she doth think to outvy me by reason of her to[o] much money, but shee is very much mistaken, I will assure thee.

I have not else at present, but my respects to you, by reason of your faithfulness towards a husband in the end. Find not fault with me.

He added a postscript: 'I hope, Mistress Bett, you will come to yourself on[e] time or another.'

One wonders what went on in that Devon household when Johnson finally returned home. If he ever did, how did he behave to Tobias and William, and the new baby, if it survived? Did Mistress Bett ever 'come to her senses' or did she continue to cling to her mother?

Before we leave the children and approach the wicked stepmother from another angle, let us just take a sidelong look at a couple of orphans and see how difficult it could be for those who were left to look after them to take the parental role.

The year after Tobias Wyseman left his children to the tender mercies of a stepfather, in the busy London parish of St Martin-in-the-Fields, John Hitson was coming to the end of twelve long years of caring for two orphan girls, as administrator of the estate of their father, Ralph Barnes. The original grant had appointed him in conjunction with one Samuel Barnes, perhaps the children's uncle or grandfather, but Barnes disappears from the scene and may have died. Hitson, probably a family friend, was left to deal with the problems that arose from the affairs of the two girls. The only evidence left of his task is the administrator's account which he rendered to the Prerogative when he finally relinquished his considerable burden.

There are sinister hints in that account, but we can only guess at what went on.

Parnell Barnes, the elder of the two girls was baptised in St Martin's in 1644, which made her about fourteen when her father died. Her sister, Mary was younger. There is no mention of Parnell by name anywhere in the account, until the end when Hitson finally pays her the £220 share of her father's money. The first item on Hitson's list of expenses, dated December 1658, is 1s. for slippers for Mary. The second is 3s. for coach hire to Bedlam, 'on the minor's occasion'. Someone had locked one of them up, it seems, or perhaps both. Was it Hitson himself or somebody else after the Barnes wealth? In January 1659 Hitson got a warrant for the arrest of Jonathan Viner who, with his wife, was keeping Mary away from him. Were the Viners a kindly couple who were trying to rescue the little girl from the cruel Hitson?

A month later, on 15 February, Joseph Hitson again took a coach and rumbled out through Bishopsgate to the grim medieval building which housed London's lunatics. This time, as requested, he was taking some toys to his little charge.

Two days later 'Aunt Barnes' appeared at Doctors' Commons, bought some clothes for the child and, accompanied by a nurse, took Mary to Southwark. From there Mary and the nurse, Anne Blake, boarded a wagon which took them down to Ashtead, where Mistress Blake lived. The Viners were evidently still trying to get hold of Mary; at the end of March a porter was paid 5s. for going to Ashtead to prevent the nurse from letting her go to them.

For the next six years there are regular payments to the nurse in Ashtead and for Hitson to go down for occasional visits. Mary's board and lodging only cost the estate £9 a year but she was kept in fine clothes. In September 1659 Hitson paid out 18s. for a coat laced with silk and silver lace and a red petticoat 'laced twice about'.

Meanwhile Hitson was busy about other affairs of the estate. Ralph Barnes had lent money for the Royalist cause and to that most impecunious of men, Lord Wentworth, Lord of the Manor of Stepney. Various arrest warrants were issued for those who had owed Barnes money and expeditions had to be made to recover debts from different parts of the country.

In May 1665 Mary was sent off to Hackney, where Mistress Freeman ran a school. Payments for petticoats, smocks, suits and serges were now sent to Hackney. She went home to the nurse for her holidays, but now she was older Hitson did not go to the expense of hiring a carriage. When she returned to school for her first autumn term one Daniel Hopkins was paid to take her on the back of his horse. He lent her 1*s*. 8*d*. because she had not money.

On Restoration Day 1667 Mary's trunk was fetched back from Hackney for the last time and, with the 2*s*. paid for that and the £220 for the mysterious Parnell, Hitson closed his account.

There were many, many orphans around, especially after the losses in the Civil War and the Plague. At least little Mary Barnes had someone to take her toys when she was confined in Bedlam and perhaps a kindly woman to look after her in Ashtead. Maybe it was better to be cared for by a well-paid stranger than to suffer the cruelties of a resentful stepparent. Perhaps it is still.

It is time to leave the weeping girls in their pigeon lofts and madhouses and consider another source of hatred and litigation in the family, the fortune-hunting wife.

Gold-diggers and good-time girls

Ten years or so after Mary Barnes had waved goodbye to her friends at Mistress Freeman's establishment in Hackney, there was a flurry of excitement at the school when a prostitute called Lucy Hungate abducted one of the girls for some nefarious purpose. Lucy was a Restoration woman of fighting spirit, who, in the 1680s, took on the establishment, suing her MP lover's family for his money.

It is fashionable in these days of the decline of the patriarchal society to see man as the oppressor and woman as the helpless victim. So far, we have rather gone along with that. We have seen Charles Pepys and Stoney Bowes at their battering and some men at the 'court of scolds' using their wives to punish their neighbours. We have even put in a good word for the wicked stepmother. But the desirable woman, armed with the glitter of youth, had immense power. Powdered and perfumed she might set out to get for herself, by hook or by crook, the financial rewards of her charms. There were better ways of doing it than by charging a guinea a night.

'In Oliver's day' [the Interregnum], said one of the witnesses at the Commons, 'He doth well remember . . . marriages were solemnized in divers ways, some by Justices of the Peace, in houses privately, others by dissenting Ministers and some according to the book of Common Prayer'.

For about a hundred years after the Restoration, marriages might still be conducted in a rather irregular fashion, in out of the way places — the marriage shops round the Fleet prison did a good trade and bigamy was rife. All that led to a good deal of uncertainty as to who was entitled to a man's estate when he died, especially if he had not left a will.

In the 1670s and 1680s interest causes flooded into the Prerogative, conducted by women who claimed marriage to men who had not left wills, and contested by their blood relatives. Many of them were women of ill repute who may or may not have gone through some form of ceremony with their lover.

However fluid the state of marriage, the law's respect for a widow's rights was very great. As we have seen, she was, by this time, almost invariably preferred to any other claimant as administratrix. Her rights of dower and free bench had been closely protected for many hundreds of years and now that the old customs were eroded there were laws in their place. The increasingly popular marriage settlement tied the real estate up in such a way that she was generously provided for. The new Statute of Distributions put the widow's traditional entitlement to a third of her husband's personal estate on to a firm legal basis. A fortune huntress had only to prove to the Civilians that she was truly married to the intestate and she could walk off with the sealed parchment which allowed her half his cash and goods, if there were no children, a third if there were.

Lucy Hungate's suit, though rather more spectacular than most, was one of many such wrangles. The case went on for at least thirteen years; there were proceedings in the Consistory as well as the Prerogative and an appeal went to the High Court of Delegates. The man in question, Sir Chichester Wray, a bachelor of thirty-three, had been returned as MP for Grimsby in 1675 to replace Gervase Holles. Four years later he contracted smallpox and died. There followed a battle royal between his mistress/wife, Lucy Hungate, his mother, Lady Olympia, and his brother and heir-at-law, Sir William.

Chichester Wray was a rake and Lucy a good-time girl from the slums round St Giles. She was twenty-four when Wray died and had been living with him since she was twenty. His estate at Ashby cum Fenby in Nottinghamshire was said to be worth £1,700 a year, although it was heavily mortgaged. When the ermine-clad advocates debated the truth of the various pleas and depositions, there was a very rough crowd of witnesses in court, and not all of them were cheering Lucy on.

Rebecca Salvin, a procuress who sold ox cheek, told fortunes and 'made matches' in a cellar near St Martin in the Fields, swore for Lucy. Her sister Jane came to court, a 'lewd, infamous and incontinent' thief of 'evil and scandalous conversation . . . a frequenter of brothels [who] hath been seen naked in bed with several men . . . hath one or more bastards'. The Wrays produced a common soldier, a coffee-house keeper who went by a variety of names and, deposing for both parties, were a whole gang of folk from Kentish Town.

Lady Olympia spat out her allegation with a venom which has defied the erosive effects of time. Lucy Hungate has been a 'common strumpet and a whore' between four and ten years. She has lived in brothels and had carnal knowledge of and the use of the bodies of several men. She has cheated the local tradesmen and used a variety of different names. She was indicted at King's Bench for taking a young girl away from a school in Hackney. Before she took up with Sir Chichester she was kept by some man near the Temple. With Wray she lived in many different lodgings, pretending to be his wife. When he was out hunting or at bowls she would 'drink and play the whore'. He contracted the clap and the French pox from her and used the services of her sister, Jane, as much as he used Lucy.

There was no question of a marriage between the two having been contracted. What Hungate has described to the court as her wedding breakfast was nothing more than an ordinary supper party. Some venison had been sent up from the country, it is true, and the whore was, indeed, presiding at table, but she was dressed in her usual fashion, not in wedding finery.

Sir Chichester had every intention of marrying Alderman Dashwood's well-dowered daughter; he was not fool enough to allow himself to be trapped again by a fortune hunter. He had said as much to a friend who had enquired if he was married: 'No, I am not married to her, know better things. The burnt child dreads the fire. I have suffered sufficiently for marrying a whore in France; I am not mad enough to marry another whore . . . here in England'.

Lucy, calling herself Dame Lucy Wray, a gentlewoman, daughter of Henry Hungate of Norfolk, Esquire, told the examiner that she had lived with Sir Chichester for several years at Mr Gettins's in Henrietta Street, at Lady Barrington's in Piccadilly and a number of other places. They had taken vows to each other and, as they regarded themselves as married in the eyes of God, she gave out to the other lodgers that they were man and wife. She had even been with him to his country mansion near Newark where his mother lived. It had been his firm intention to oust Lady Olympia from Ashby and install Lucy there instead. She and her maid took a coach to Newark and Sir Chichester joined them after a few days. He then went off to the house to see if the coast was clear, and, finding his mother gone, sent for Lucy.

Some short time after the excursion to Ashby in 1679 a wedding was planned. The couple bought a wedding ring 'without a posy . . . as was the fashion for wedding rings' from the jeweller, Hamersley (the ring was produced in court as an exhibit), and a venison pasty was ordered for the celebratory meal. Off they went to Kentish Town to be married by the vicar there, Randolph Yarwood, but were apparently unable to find him. They had more success the following day. On 11 July 1679, Sir Chichester Wray took Lucy Hungate to be his lawful wedded wife, by the Book of Common Prayer, in a large room at a 'house of entertainment' at the Spring Garden near Knightsbridge. Or so she said. The landlord of the house was called Swindall and the vicar of Kentish town officiated.

As might be expected, the vicar's evidence was crucial and his reputation of vital importance to the court's decision. That was the occasion of the ale-house keepers, housewives and labourers of Kentish Town coming to the Commons. Randolph Yarwood, claimed Lady Olympia, was of 'loose, scandalous and evil life . . . much given to excessive drinking, fighting and quarrelling

. . . a great disturber of the peace and quiet of his neighbours', a vexatious litigant and a fraud. The Dean and Chapter of St Paul's had suspended him a few years ago for conducting a marriage without banns or licence. He was often involved in tithe suits with his parishioners and the Wrays were sure that Lucy had bribed him; he had been seen conferring with her proctors and advocates.

When taking the Sunday service at St Pancras Church, the congregation often noticed that Yarwood was drunk and not able to tell whether it was 'sermon' or a burial he was conducting. There had been occasions at funerals when 'he hath not been able to speak a plain word, nor to stand, but hath reeled and staggered at the graves'. Mistress Keat, whose first husband Yarwood had buried four years since, said it was nonsense, and Elizabeth French who kept an alehouse about a mile from the church said she had never seen him in drink. This was confirmed by the widow who kept the alehouse which Yarwood frequented.

There were some obvious inconsistencies in Lucy's story and Yarwood was notorious. For reasons which should not be ascribed to discrimination against female low life, the judges eventually found for the Wray family. Lady Olympia had died in the meantime and Sir William was still struggling to sort out his brother's estate in 1707. Lucy was excommunicated for not paying her lawyer, although she managed to extricate herself subsequently, perhaps from the pocket of another client!

St Pancras Old Church, where the Reverend Randolph Yarwood 'reeled and staggered at the graves.' (The Guildhall Library, London)

With a passing look into the Court of Arches, where the family of young John Moore, 'of weak parts and mightily accustomed and addicted to drinking', were fighting the claim of a barmaid who had trapped him into marriage, we will leave London with the vicar of Kentish Town hiccuping round his churchyard and take coach for Buckinghamshire.

It is a late November afternoon in 1702 when we arrive in the village of Fawley, three miles from Henley on Thames. If we look in through the windows at the rectory, before the maid draws the curtains against the fading winter light, we will see the minister, Mr John Franklin, cosy at his fireside, in conversation with an elderly lady parishioner. The subject of their conversation, and the talk of the village, is old Weedon of Bosmear Manor, who was buried a few days before.

'It would have vexed you, if you had bin heire to such an Estate', said the minister, 'to have a soldier's widow run away with it'. Time and again, he added, he had pressed the old man to make a will, but he had not done so. He had said as much at the funeral; 'I vow to God, it is a sad thing that a man should dye without making a will'.

He was not alone. Robert Weedon was a timber merchant in a considerable way of business, said to be worth £12,000. Until recently he had been single. A remote relative called Cavendish Weedon had brought him a will form and tried to get him to fill it in. Another, Thomas Weedon of London, had often waited on the old man with his wife and child to the same purpose and had sent him bottles of wine as an inducement. Nine months before he died, when he was senile and 'became a Child and easy to be rul'd', he married a 'lusty proper woman', a widow by the name of Frances Dowcett.

It was generally agreed in the drinking establishments of Fawley, Henley, Marlow and Fair Mile End that Dowcett was after Weedon's money. The clientele and staff in the local taverns and alehouse were in a good position to know what went on in the Weedon household, for the old man seems to have spent most of his time downing ale in the congenial atmosphere of the undemanding taproom. In spite of his wealth and status as a former sheriff and tax commissioner, he 'was better pleased with low company than gentlemen and . . . drank with porters and labouring men'. Sometimes he was so drunk that he had to be put to bed by the landlord and soaked the mattress right through.

When the drink finally finished Robert Weedon off, Thomas Weedon appears to have got together with some of his alehouse cronies and a will was concocted. Or, maybe, as the Civilians seem to have believed, the old man had truly made a will which he kept secret from his wife. Naturally the widow disputed it and suits rattled round Doctors' Commons for several years, in the Prerogative and before the Delegates. A will of the real estate was tried before the Lord Chief Justice of Common Pleas at Westminster; the widow was turned out of her house, got back in and then again it was repossessed.

The evidence for the Prerogative's case was taken in Henley by commission in the April of 1704, eighteen months after the old man's death and six months after the case was heard in Westminster. The witnesses, most of whom had been up to London for the business at Common Pleas, were sworn one afternoon in the parish church. The next day everyone went off to the Bell to be questioned. Proceedings went on for three days, starting every morning at seven; twenty-four witnesses were called, an astonishing array of locals, publicans, barmaids, distillers, farmers, carpenters, a butcher, a harness maker, a malster. Even the rector's daughter turned up to confirm that a will had been made; she denied that old Weedon had ever 'paid court to her' or that Thomas Weedon had bribed her with 'linnen, scarves, hoods, stockings or other things.' She was asked, for reasons which are not immediately apparent, whether or not she was a virgin.

The widow's case was, predictably, that on the occasion when the will was supposed to have been made, Weedon was drunk. He had been drinking all day at the Catherine Wheel in Henley with his old friend, William Hellier. About ten o'clock Hellier, who had been trying for hours to persuade Weedon to make a will, led him off to the riverside wharf where he usually tethered his horse when he was in town. The old man had done 'the deeds of Nature in his Breeches' and kept falling over. Hellier decided to take him to the Bell where, he said, he had a couple of fowl which they would eat for supper. A will was, supposedly drawn: someone reported that Weedon staggered down the stairs into the inn yard, demanding, 'Prithee, man, where is that silly will thou talkest of?'

The lawyers on both sides went to extreme lengths to discredit the opponents' witnesses. Elizabeth Havergill, a barmaid, was produced to blacken Hellier. She had a phenomenal memory, or perhaps it was invention. Twelve years before, she said, Hellier had come to the Greyhound, which she had at that time run with her mother. He had with him one Besse Pink who was supposedly a 'kinswoman from London'. The couple took an upstairs room and had wine and potted pigeon for supper. After they had dined Hellier locked Elizabeth in a room somewhere. Elizabeth escaped and, looking through the keyhole in her bedchamber door, spied Besse Pink and Hellier in bed together with a candle flickering on the stool by the bed.

Barbara Wiggins, who kept the Nine of Diamonds at Fair Mile End, said that she had been got at before the Common Pleas trial by Thomas Weedon's supporters. The lawyers suggested that her credibility was dubious because it was rumoured that her husband had left her because he feared she was trying to do away with him with rat poison.

There was much talk of people being bribed with 'fat sides of hogs' among other things. One of the witnesses had run off to the West Indies to escape his creditors and another was said to be 'a poor broken indigent fellow . . . drawne by gaine to swear anything'. Thomas Commins's testimony was held to be worthless because he, as a Poll Tax Assessor, had falsified his own returns and concealed the existence of his large family.

The Court's final decision, confirmed a year later by the Delegates, was that the will produced should be upheld. There it still lies, among the thousands of others, with the seal of approval on it, witness to an old man's first love, drink. There is no reference to the lusty widow. Thomas Weedon takes the residue, but there is an important 40*s.* a year for the ostler at the Bell in Henley.

Fathers

The closest blood relationships, when soured, poisoned or warped, turn into the most searing of hatreds. A father's mixed feelings for the children who come to displace him have been well attested since the Greeks invented their terrible god Kronos. Worse than the unhappy resentments of step-relationships are the tales from the Commons of parent–child affections gone awry. The most notorious of unnatural fathers in the annals of the Prerogative happen to be two very celebrated Englishmen, the poet John Milton, the scrivener's son, and the architect Sir John Soane.

Milton's first marriage, to Mary Powell, in June 1642, was unhappy; the couple separated almost immediately, but were reconciled in an uneasy and bitter relationship. The liaison produced four children, a son who died, three daughters who survived, and a tract advocating divorce. The £1,000 promised to Milton under the terms of the marriage settlement never materialised and that is said to have contributed to the bad feelings between father and daughters. His contempt for women as subordinate and inferior beings and the severe domestic regime which the blind autocratic Puritan imposed on his all female household must have made the Milton home a dreadful place.

Mary had died in 1652 leaving Anne, six, Mary, four and Deborah, a baby. Four years later Milton married Catherine Woodcock, who lived for only fifteen months. Seven years later he took his last spouse, Elizabeth Minshull, who seems to have played her domestic role in an obedient and dutiful way, which annoyed her husband less than her predecessors had done.

In the year leading up to his own death from gout, twenty years after the first fateful marriage, Milton often spoke of the disposal of his estate. His brother remembered and subsequently wrote down what he had said one particular summer's day. The curt, cruel note was later produced at the Prerogative as a nuncupative or reported will:

> Memorandum that John Milton, late of the parish of St Giles,
> Cripplegate . . . did at several times before his death and in particular on
> or about the 26th day of July . . . declare his will and intent as to the
> disposall of his estate in the words following or to that or like effect.
> The portion due to me from Mr Powell my former wife's father I leave
> to the unkind Children I had by her, haveing receiv'd no parte of it, but
> my meaning is they shall have no other benefit from my estate then the
> said portion and what I shall have besides done for them, they having
> been very undutifull to me. All the residue of my estate I leave to the
> disposall of Elizabeth, my loveing wife.

The girls, all in their twenties, contested the will, claiming, rightly, that the £1,000 dowry was an irrecoverable debt. Two servant girls, the Fisher sisters, one of whom was employed in the Milton household, were sent to the Commons by Milton's widow and her brother-in-law, to repeat vicious tittle-tattle about relationships in the family in support of the 'will'. Elizabeth Fisher's account was soon as well known as *Paradise Lost*:

> [She] hath heard the deceased declare his displeasure against the parties
> Ministrant, his children and, particularly the deceased declared to this
> Respondent, that a little before he was married to Elizabeth Milton, his
> now Relict, a former Maidservant of his told Mary, one of the
> Deceased's daughters . . . that she heard the deceased was to be
> married. To which the said Mary replied . . . that that was noe News to
> heare of his wedding, but if shee could heare of his death, that was
> something.

The angry girl was fifteen when her father married for the third time; unfortunate that she had the news of her father's forthcoming nuptials from a servant!

The maid went on: 'The deceased . . . further told this Respondent that all his said Children did combine together and counsell his Maidservant to cheat him . . . in her markettings.'

If the maids are to be believed, and one must always remember they were probably bribed by the widow, the girls' bitterness against their grim misogynist father was honed to a fine edge. Perhaps it was just his paranoia: 'The deceased . . . said that his Children had made away some of his bookes and would have sold the rest of his bookes to the Dunghill women'.

Neither of the servant girls was able to think of anything that Milton had done for his daughters in his lifetime, except that he had 'bred up' the lame and unmarriageable Anne to the trade of gold and silver lace-making.

The widow's lawyers, having demonstrated the ill will between father and daughters, led the witnesses to say something about the love between Milton and his wife. The opposition had evidently suggested that his painful gout had put him into a 'passion or angry humour' with Mistress Milton. All the lawyers could muster were two statements supposedly made by the poet when he was dining with his wife. One day in July she had cooked a dish which he relished . . . 'God have mercy, Betty', he remarked, quite in character, 'I see thou wilt performe according to thy promise in providing mee such dishes as I think fitt whilst I live, and when I dye thou knowest I have left thee all'.

A month before he died, as he was eating a midday meal in the kitchen of the house at the Artillery Ground, Mary Fisher heard him say: 'Make much of mee as long as I live, for thou knowest I have given thee all when I die at thy disposall'.

The evidence was too slim to allow a will which disinherited lawful children to stand. Elizabeth Milton was made administratrix, which meant she was, under the recent statute, obliged to hand over two-thirds of the personal estate to Mary, Anne and Deborah. She did not; each got a paltry £100, from an estate of £1,500. Releases were signed which absolved the stepmother from further obligation. Perhaps Milton's daughters were grateful to get anything at all.

Milton's shortcomings as a father of daughters sprang from the disaster of his marriage to their mother, compounded by his resentment against his in-laws. Behind that lay the deep abyss of fear and hatred which often divides the sexes. The poet is thought to have written *Samson Agonistes*, the tragedy of woman as betrayer, the year after his first little girl was born.

Poor lame Anne Milton is at her bobbins, as we leave Restoration London and come forward in time to the year the young Victoria ascended the throne. It is January and the trees in Lincoln's Inn Fields are stark. The grand house at number twelve is hushed; the master has departed this life, leaving his collection of cold antiquities to the nation.

In the yellow drawing-room of Sir John Soane's house, which still has its elegant eighteenth-century decorations, there hangs, just to the left of the fireplace, a painting of two fine young gentlemen. One is dark and rather drawn-looking; the other is ruddier and seems to have more life in him. They are the sons of the household: John, the elder is the pale one, dead long before his father; the other is George, the scapegrace. He will soon be at the Commons fighting for something more than the small allocation made to him from the

George Soane (left), with his elder brother John at Cambridge, by W Owen. (By courtesy of the Trustees of Sir John Soane's Museum, London)

estate of his immensely wealthy father, some recompense, perhaps for years of spiteful disregard.

Sir John Soane's loathing for his younger son was no secret. It was the talk of London. Soane's biographer writes of George's 'pathological hostility to his parents'. The origins of the trouble between George and his father lay, in all probability, in the humble Buckinghamshire cottage where the young architect, John Soane, had struggled to equip himself for escape. He was born in poverty and ignomimy and never spoke of his childhood. There is no mention of his father in his letters and diaries, although his mother was proudly dressed up and had her portrait painted along with the rest of the family. Soane senior is said to have been a Goring bricklayer, but it has not been proven and it is worth considering the possibility that Sir John may have been illegitimate himself. Something about the circumstances of George's birth and the events surrounding it may have triggered off some buried anxiety in the father. Who can say what that volatile and much-hated man saw when he looked into his baby's face?

His will left the residue of his estate to the children of his elder son; he had already left his house and collection of antiques to the nation by private Act of Parliament. For George, there was a very small annuity. The case papers in the Prerogative and the bundles of letters in the museum in Lincoln's Inn Fields tell a sad story.

Sir John Soane, the self-made man, in his Masonic dress, by John Jackson. (By courtesy of the Trustees of Sir John Soane's Museum, London)

John was born in 1786, his brother four years later. Their father was already astonishingly successful, a self-made man who rose from nothing to be the most highly acclaimed architect in the country. Elizabeth Soane was ill after George's birth and he was put out to wet-nurse with a journeyman bricklayer's wife. The nurse, Mrs Leake, lost her own baby soon after this and clung to little George. However, Mrs Soane discovered that the nurse was 'addicted to the use of intoxicating liquours and improper foods'. She tried to reclaim the child, but the nurse refused to relinquish him until she was forced to do so by the Court of Conscience in Piccadilly.

From then on George's father 'conceived and ever after entertained and frequently expressed an insane notion or delusion that the said George Soane was not his child, but that of his nurse'. There were public rows between Soane and his adored wife on the subject.

There are only hints in the Soane papers of how Sir John behaved towards his children in their early years. His famous notebook mentions an occasion when George was helping him to catalogue his library and the boy flew into a rage and hurled the inkwell to the floor. In July 1798 Sir John noted: 'Paid to Mr Wicks for keeping the children in ignorance, ½ year £39 13s. 0d.'.

When he was seventeen, George went to Cambridge and, as students will, especially those with rich fathers, ran up some debts. They were not astronomical and his allowance, which the father claimed was 'unlimited' was a mean £5 a term. Unlike his brother, who left university through ill health, George persevered. His father had determined that he should study medicine; his inclinations were elsewhere and he begged to be allowed to continue with his study of law. His request was refused and he was put by his father as an apprentice to a physician where he was 'placed behind a counter to tie labels and cork bills between 12 and one every morning'.

Sir John's outrage at his son's relatively modest debts of £200 was out of all proportion, especially when one considers how much he was spending on collecting antiquities at the time. When the young man took up writing, for which he had some talent, and embarked upon an early marriage to a publisher's daughter, Agnes Boaden, his father's rage now knew no bounds. A rather pathetic note from the young man, now twenty-one, speaks volumes. He has had his first 'literary trifle' published and, with trepidation, offers it to his father with a request for an interview. One month later his father replied thus: 'Sir, I must beg to decline the interview proposed. Yours etc.'

The frosty relations between father and son declined into a vicious, public battle. George, now desperate for money, wrote begging for a little help and to be allowed to visit him: 'Permit me once more to address your feelings as a father and a man . . . It is now two years since I have been banished from your presence . . . Is it natural to consider a son as an enemy?'

Sir John replied:

> If you must continue to misapply your time, and to lose the advantage
> of an expensive education, I fear your friends can be of no use. I have
> read your publications – such productions will neither add to your fame,
> nor increase your fortune.

George's wife now had a baby and their need was great. But Sir John
was unmoved: 'In reply to your letter, in which you have noticed two person-
ages entire strangers to me, 'Agnes and her child'.'

Three years later George took his revenge and published in *The
Champion* a vitriolic attack on his father's design for the Clerk of Works's
house in Chelsea Hospital, amongst other things:

> On the top, at the back, are two large raisin jars. Let us not be
> understood to speak jestingly, we say it in all the gravity of truth, that
> there are two large raisin jars, fresh to all appearances from the grocer's
> shop: fronting them, arranged in military array, appear a little regiment
> of chimney pots with white heads, like so many well grown
> cawliflowers.

He deplores the new Bank of England his father has decorated with:

> Remnants of Mausoleums, Caryatides, Pillars from Temples, ornaments
> from the Pantheon – all heaped together with a perversion of taste that
> is truly admirable. He steals a bit there and a bit here.

> The most extraordinary instance of this perversity of taste and dulness
> of invention is to be found in the Artist's house in Lincoln's Inn Fields.
> The exterior . . . seems as if it were intended to convey a satire upon
> himself: it looks like a record of the departed, and can only mean he has
> reared this Mausoleum for the enshrinement of his body.

On the copy of the review article exhibited in the Commons to demonstrate
the extent of the acrimony, are some notes made by George's lawyer for his
speech in court:

> What provoked G S to write this? He was in jail [for debt], his wife
> confined with twins, an execution in the house, one child dies, G S
> obtains a day rule to go out and bury his infant, he thereon writes warm
> letters to his father who sends Vaux and Munro to the jail to prove him
> mad. Will not that account for it.

Worse was yet to come. Seventeen years after the *Champion* review, Sir John
penned an hysterical and libellous account of his son's life and misdeeds and
had it published. The core revelation was that George had sired a baby by his
sister-in-law. Soane had pursued the investigation of this matter with bizarre
fervour and thoroughness. The child, Manfred, had been baptised with his
'half sisters' in the church of St Mary, Southampton. The old man had the

Sir John Soane's real mausoleum, in the churchyard of St Pancras Old Church.
(Photograph: A F Kersting)

curate correct the entry in the parish register and the depositions of a doctor and another witness were sealed up and put in the parish chest.

Surely this was not just the action of a self-made man exasperated by the failure of his only surviving child to come up to his expectations? Did the famous man not, as George's proctors at the Commons suggested 'overstep the line which alone separates and distinguishes extreme eccentricity from actual mental derangement'.

The Court decided, however, that the will should stand, although the suit rumbled on in Chancery. The 'mausoleum' in Lincoln's Inn Fields is open to the public, as Soane intended it should be. One of the recent visitors there was a descendant of George, who, says the Archivist, bore a quite remarkable resemblance to the Sir John of the Lawrence portrait. So much for the architect's conviction that his hated child was a changeling.

Mothers

The wise novelist has suggested why Stoney Bowes may have beaten his wife. Barry Lyndon, Thackeray's Stoney character, speaks of his mother: 'I don't care to own that she is the only human being whom I am afraid to face. I can recollect her fits of anger as a child, and the reconciliations, which used to be still more violent and painful'.

'The principal cause of all nervous breakdown', wrote the Director of the Tavistock Clinic in the 1920s, 'lies in the wrong treatment of the child by his parents'.

> Some can pot begonias and some can bud a rose,
> And some are hardly fit to trust with anything that grows.

In previous generations, when the higher echelons of society farmed their children out to others and even the middling sort used wet-nurses, the overwhelming influence of mother on infant could not have been as great as it subsequently became. What is more, fewer children had natural mothers which survived to bring them up. Nevertheless, the hand that rocks the cradle rules the world and many mothers did rock their own babies. When the intensity of feeling which ties a boy to his mother's breast is blasted by resentment, cruelty born of her own suffering, the exercise of unrestrained power or manipulation, all hell breaks loose.

In the days when the Devil was so prone to occupy a little body and violence was the order of the day, there was plenty of opportunity for the exercise of sadism under the guise of responsible parenting. How many women, beaten by the husbands, beat their sons? For many the control of weak, dependent human beings was the only chance they had to wield the intoxicating weapon of power.

The scream of children battered by their natural parents is not something which haunts the Commons, however; by the time those children appear in court they are angry, damaged adults. Most are male, the reason being that, as the law restricts women's property rights, men are more likely than their sisters to be battling with their widowed mothers. Moreover, there seems to have been, as there still often is, a camaraderie between mothers and daughters which bound them close enough to keep the vice avarice at bay.

First there are three men whose filial stance suggests that something was lacking in their childhoods, although no questions are asked or answered as to what lay behind their unnatural behaviour.

The widow Dewes died in 1719 in Diss. In the contest over her modest estate between a son, Charles, and a grandson, Robert, the court learned some strange things about the former's behaviour. 'Of a sordid and covetous temper', and a 'fornicator', he was said to sell the left-over scraps of food from his table and go round with a jug to his neighbours, begging for beer. When his old mother died he was all for cutting off the corpse's hair and selling it and for using the floor-boards from her house to make a coffin.

Abraham Rookes's treatment of his living mother is more telling. When she lost her house in the Great Fire, the Widow Rookes took lodgings in a village near Barking. She was very frail and survived the upheaval less than a year. Abraham died soon after and there was a dispute between his executor and his daughter-in-law as to how the old woman had disposed of her money.

There had, said some of the witnesses, been no love lost between mother and son, and the daughter-in-law claimed that the old lady had made a will in Abraham's favour 'to avoid the threats of her said sonne' fearing she was in danger of her life. When he went out to Barking to visit, 'choloricke words' were overheard by the landlord's daughter. Mistress Rookes, the girl went on, 'was a very aged, weake women in her limbs . . . did goe up and downe stares with a great deale of difficulty and pains'. She would 'crawl up stairs on her hands and feet to avoyd her sonne . . . when he came into the house'.

If Rookes did manage to catch his mother, her grandson's wife said that he:

> Did use her most barbarously, inhumanely and despightfully in deeds
> and words, and did often beat, strike and kicke and most shamefully
> abuse her . . . it was usual with him to call her . . . Old Jade, damned
> bitch, damned whore, and wish that she were damned in hell, and said a
> plague confound her . . . She would and did fall into a great shaking and
> trembling.

In the same year that the Widow Rookes was creeping about on all fours in fear of her son in the village of Barking, Mary Martin, a widow with a fine three-storey house in Westminster, was going about disguised in an 'unknowne habitt' to avoid being arrested by the bailiffs who had been put up to it by her son Henry Allured to scare her.

There had evidently been trouble between the boy and his mother for some years. The previous Christmas she had 'passionately' complained to an old friend that she had placed Henry as an apprentice to a Holborn apothecary and he had taken 'ill courses and would not mind his calling'. With tears in her eyes and her hand on her breast, she protested that for his unkindness he would have no more than 'twelve pence of her estate'.

To another friend she lamented: 'Nothing doth so much grieve me as the unnaturalnes of the Child I bare with my own body'.

Henry was unemployed and of no fixed abode, had spent £300 of his mother's money and was demanding another £50.

Whilst fleeing from the bailiffs Mary went to lodge at a shoemaker's in the Strand, in the same house as her married daughter, another Mary. It was either there or in some other lodgings (opinions vary) that she fell ill and died.

The old lady had some valuable posessions, including diamonds, pearls, furs and some fine cloth of gold upholstery fabric. Diamonds worth £40 had been pawned by her late second husband to a woman in Lambeth and the other jewels had been hidden at a neighbour's when she took flight. Her house in Petty France was well furnished. The four-poster was hung with green perpetuana (a heavy woollen cloth) and yellow lace, and in the dining-room the chairs were covered with red baize and turkey work; the curtains were striped silk and there was a red carpet on the floor.

An unmarried daughter, Abigail, who had stayed at home with her mother, was quick off the mark in taking letters of administration at the Westminster court, omitting all reference to the pawned diamonds in the inventory. This was before the passing of the Statute of Distributions and she could easily have taken the lot for herself. Her impecunious brother, however, sued her in the Prerogative. It was a particularly acrimonious case, with Mary Martin's three children literally fighting over her corpse. Henry's lawyers, seeking to prove Abigail's neglect of the mother, concentrated on her conduct after the old women had died. The body, it was claimed, was left for days without burial so that it stank.

Abigail protested that it was not true. She seems to have been agitated and anxious when it came to this part of her allegation and repeated herself. A day or two after her mother's death:

> The body was cleansed and taken away, and that, other than purging, which happened a day or two after her death, there was no savour at all arising from her. [She] was an old thinne, lean dry person, and that when she was stript and costynned [sic], and some few hours before she was buried . . . her body was a leane and thinne corps and sweet and gave no offence, nor was noisome at all.

The main burden of Abigail's evidence was an attack on her brother for his cruelty to their mother with some remarks about Mary's refusal to bother with her. While she, Abigail, 'did carry and demeane herselfe . . . as a dutifull and loving daughter, and was very observant, careful and tender of and attendant upon her . . . and very serviceable unto her', Mary left the dying woman 'sick upon her bed . . . [she] ranne up and down to see shewes'. When asked for help she would snap: 'Get you home and be hanged to your dutifull daughter'.

All that dirty linen was washed in public to no avail. The case was settled out of court and a creditor took administration. The old lady had been badly in debt; her diamonds had been pawned, her lodger had run off without paying the rent and she was frightened enough of the bailiffs to leave home and go about in disguise.

One can only speculate as to what the mothers of Diss, Barking and Westminster had done to cause their sons to treat them as they did. The case of Lady Chapman and her son, James, is different. The estate in dispute was considerable and the parties were high ranking. Very many people of substance brought their opinions to the Commons and much evidence survives to document the relationship between mother and son.

As ever, there are divergent accounts, but it is surely not fanciful to see in the character of James Chapman, as described by his friends, a deeply depressed, disturbed man, grown from a bullied and unloved child.

Winter came early in 1698; there was a snow fall at the end of October. It is the evening of the last Sunday of the month, and we are in St John's Street, Clerkenwell. Through the fog two figures can just be distinguished slipping along the icy street carrying a sedan chair. Two men emerge from one of the houses, and one of them, well muffled against the cold, is helped into the chair. He is young, but, has difficulty supporting himself and the lamplight flickers on a pale face and dances out of wild, staring eyes. James Chapman, aged twenty-seven, the eldest son of Sir John Chapman, former Lord Mayor of London, deceased, has only a month left of his unhappy life.

On this wintry night his apothecary is taking him off to dine with the 'best friend he had in the world' Simon Folkes, forty-eight, gentleman, of Hatton Garden and Woodford. It is only a quarter of a mile, at the most, to Folkes's house, but his doctor said it was madness to take him out on a night like this, 'enough to kill him'. The next day the sick man will sit 'in a Chatte by the fireside in the little parlour' in Hatton Garden and make a will leaving virtually everything to his friend Folkes. The contest between Lady Chapman and Folkes is to cause a great stir in legal circles in the City of London.

James's father has been dead for nearly ten years. 'A firm and hearty Protestant', he was Lord Mayor for a few brief troubled months at the very time of the bloodless coup which came to be known as the Glorious Revolution. Whilst trying the monstrous Judge Jeffries he had a stroke from which he died. A modest, charitable and scrupulously honest man, he was said to be a 'tender and provident father', 'a good Neighbour, and a hearty friend . . . a general lover of mankind'.

Thus proclaimed Dr John Scott at his funeral, at the end of a thunderous sermon on the theme of death being better than life, black with passionate, pessimistic rhetoric. James, eighteen, and down from Cambridge for his father's obsequies, sitting in the fine new church of St Lawrence Jewry, with his mother, younger brother and two sisters, can have drawn little comfort from the tirade:

Griefs, Troubles and Diseases twist themselves about our Life, as the Ivy about the Oak, till they have exhausted all the Sap of it.

How many are oppressed with Slavery, harass'd with Cruelty, pined with Want and Poverty, overwhelmed with Shame and Infamy . . . wasted with long sicknesses, outworn with lingering Pains, consumed with Vexation, Sorrow and Anxiety of Soul . . . stung with Remorse, rackt with Horrour and Despair, alarmed with perpetual Fears and dismal Expectations.

Lady Chapman was said to have preferred her younger son, 'her Darling', to her elder, and there are strong intimations that she had ill-treated James in some way or other. There is no evidence as to where Sir John's preferences lay or what sort of a father he was behind closed doors. We know that he sent James presents while he was at Cambridge and that he left the bulk of his estate to his eldest son, but that was only to be expected. We can only guess at how James reacted to the loss of his father and what his behaviour was for the next eight years, but by 1697 he was certainly in a diagnosable state of depression. If the evidence of a number of respectable gentlemen and merchants is to be believed, James saw his mother as the cause of his 'melancholy'. If anyone was ever 'alarmed with perpetual Fears and dismal Expectations', he was.

In 1694 he bought a clerkship in the *nisi prius* office of King's Bench from Simon Folkes and appears to have spent his time in Gray's Inn, where the offices were, at the Exchange and in the coffee houses and taverns in the vicinity. His drinking companions were all men considerably older than himself. Some time in the late 1690s he moved out of the family mansion in Broad Street, according to some to get away from Lady Chapman, and took lodgings in St Paul's Churchyard.

According to Ford, who kept a coffee house in Cloth Fair which James frequented, as well as to others, legal colleagues and friends, he became inordinately attached to Folkes and said he was 'a father to him'. An anxious, nervous young man, whose face 'clouded over in the company of strangers', he derived comfort and even joy from his closeness to the older man and became uneasy when he was out of town. On many occasions Ford had, at James's behest, sent messengers off to try and find his friend for him.

One day in early June 1697, James was dining with Marmaduke Proctor, a city Grocer, in the Three Cranes tavern in Poultry, when he collapsed. Some said it was a stroke. An apothecary was called to attend to him and Proctor begged James to go to his mother's house, which was nearby. He refused, saying that 'his mother would have Deputy Langham, hee having bin used to their family or their Apothecary'.

Dr Ralph Hicks, physician to Lady Chapman and her family, was sent for and James was taken home to Broad Street and put under his mother's care. His condition was so alarming that Dr Edward Tyson was summoned from Bedlam. Hicks, Tyson and the family surgeon, who bled him, agreed that he was 'in a very great rage and a distracted condition'. Tyson said he was as bad as any of the patients he had confined in the Bethlehem Hospital. Sometimes James seemed unable to speak and at others would scream and roar, 'under a great fright and apprehension' that 'some mischief would be done to him'. For sixteen days they had to keep continual watch for fear he should harm himself.

The frightened servants (who saw James daily during this time), and family visitors presented a united front to the court. James Chapman was mad. There were reports that he had periods of being 'melancholy and dozy', he heard voices and noises, especially the rustling of paper when there was none. When his aunt visited he was restless and agitated; sitting first in one chair, then suddenly starting up, he would move to another and beat his elbows violently on the arms, and then get up again and walk round the room.

Some nights he would not sleep at all but rushed up and down stairs making so much noise that the watch would knock on the door and ask if anything was amiss. His paranoia was frightful to behold; so convinced was he that 'they' were out to get him, so anguished was his terror, that his brother suggested they post a man with a blunderbuss at his bedroom door to put his mind at rest. He was convinced that he had heard two neighbours 'contriving against him'.

Two of the servants reported references to Folkes in his ravings that sit ill with the report of the keeper of Ford's coffee house, and sound too contrived to ring true: 'Folkes was killed and there was an end of a rogue, for hee had ruined many a young man and got him into bonds'.

One of Lady Chapman's maids said that he 'hooped and bellowed' and said he had heard the halberds come with Folkes and they were killing him in Round Court, 'meaning' said she, 'a Court against the windows of the Roome where he lay'. Another servant heard him call 'Bring the bonds here'.

The medical advisers recommended a rest-cure in the country and James was sent off to Richmond for the end of the summer. He returned to London, apparently *compos mentis,* and changed his lodgings. It was the Saturday before Shrove Tuesday when one Freeman went to Hester Browne's lodging house in St John's Street (where we first met Chapman) to make the arrangements. James himself then appeared and paid the 2*s.* 6*d.* deposit, for a dining-room and a bedchamber which he was to rent at 6*s.* a week. According to the landlady, James was quite in charge of his affairs. Freeman, who moved into the lodgings at the same time as James, was a companion who shared a pipe and a drink with him at the end of the evening.

Lady Chapman's lawyers would argue that James was still distracted and that Freeman was his 'keeper', a man in the pay of Folkes. His job was to guard the sick man, get him drunk as much as possible to ensure that his conditioned worsened, so that Folkes, exploiting the young man's dependence on him, might get hold of his fortune.

Once the half-crown deposit was paid and the two men had moved their belongings in, they went off and did not reappear for six months. Almost as soon as they had gone a fine lady applied to Mistress Browne for lodgings. Whilst she was being shown round she enquired who lived on the first floor and was told that it was James and Freeman. She departed without engaging a room and the landlady noticed, as she got into her coach, that it bore the same coat of arms as she had seen on James's belongings. Lady Chapman was snooping around to find out what had happened to her son.

He had gone to stay in Folkes's country mansion in the pleasant Essex village of Woodford, either taking himself off for another rest-cure, or kidnapped.

Folkes's witnesses, lawyers, representatives of coffee house and tavern society and members of the wealthy 'commuting' set who had country houses in Walthamstow and Woodford were questioned as to the circumstances of James's stay and as to his state of mind, both when he was at Woodford and before. As far as they could see he had free run of Folkses's house, full command of the servants and two horses in the stable. He would often take his meals at the White Horse inn, and Folkes's gardener said he remembered taking him fresh salad there and 'a dozen of the best Apricocks'.

As to his mental condition, there were occasional 'passions' as there had been before, when he opened a bill or his dinner was late, or when his mother was spoken of, but they abated as soon as the cause of them was removed. He was a regular sufferer from 'green sickness' (anaemia) which, according to Henry Wynne, an elderly Clothmaker of Chancery Lane, 'he did attribute . . . to be occasioned to [his mother's] unkindness to him'.

James told Marmaduke Proctor, with whom he had been dining when he collapsed the previous summer, that his mother had already tried to defraud him out of part of his father's estate. She falsified accounts and took all the rent for the houses in Milk Street when she was only entitled to one-third.

James seemed to benefit from his stay in Woodford; he told Robert Russel, an old friend of Folkes's, that 'he thought he would be well soon, if it was not for the disturbance and uneasily [sic] he had in his mind from his mother'.

Events at Woodford were, naturally, portrayed in quite a different way by the opposition. A distant relative who happened to go to the house with a friend who was thinking of buying it, chanced to meet James walking in the gardens with his 'keeper'. Freeman, he said, 'stood behind [James], and did speake often to him and had an awe and Government over him'. The Irish nurse, who seems to have been in attendance some of the time, said that he was kept drugged with alcohol and was 'very melancholy and did not have the use of his reason'.

James stayed at Woodford from May till October and then, with Freeman in tow, went back to Clerkenwell where he fell into a physical decline and died within a couple of months; tuberculosis was diagnosed as the cause of death. The will which, according to Lady Chapman, was the purpose of the expedition through the snow in the sedan chair, left his residue and bulk of his estate to Folkes, with a derisory £10 for his mother. He or his warders must have had second thoughts subsequently, as there is a codicil dated three weeks after the will was made, whereby he leaves a further £30 to Lady Chapman.

Two days after James died, Folkes and his brother and a group of lawyers and friends met in the King's Head tavern on the corner of Chancery Lane and Fleet Street for the opening of the will. It was sealed with James's seal and wrapped in a piece of paper with his name on it.

Battle commenced. Batteries of lawyers and witnesses assembled at the Commons to debate James Chapman's state of mind. Was he a neurotic and insecure man whose only comforter was the kindly Folkes, or was he a schizophrenic captured by an unscrupulous band of villains? Certainly Folkes was in financial trouble, his house was mortgaged and up for sale; he had been engaged in some questionable deals. The Chapman millions would have come in handy.

There does not seem to be any doubt that during the time he was kept in his mother's house in the summer of 1697 James Chapman was manic. The three medical witnesses, Hicks, Tyson and Langham, the family apothecary, had reputations to protect and their evidence must be taken at its face value. But none of them had treated him thereafter and Dr Cox, who had, told the court that James's behaviour during his terminal illness was simply that of a physically sick man, 'fretful and peevish'. Cox's evidence was supported by James's own apothecary. The conduct which the Irish nurse describes, even though she was one of Lady Chapman's witnesses, was that of a tetchy neurotic, dying of consumption, not a raving lunatic. He refused to put on the shirt which she had warmed for him, called her and his landlady 'bitches and jades' and threatened to kick them downstairs.

The will was never proved, but you can see it in the records of the probate court, bearing the Chapman seal and with its paper cover, still labelled in a very shaky hand: 'James Chapman, my will'. The Civilians evidently decided that the family's entitlement to the Lord Mayor's estate should take priority over the dubious claims of his son's 'best friend in the world'. Their task, ultimately, was not to judge James Chapman's relationship with his mother, but to decide on the validity of a will, executed under suspicious circumstances, which went against nature.

Article 38 of the interrogatories which Folkes's proctors had drawn to be asked of Lady Chapman's witnesses was a question about her ladyship's attitude to her elder son. All of them answered, predictably, that 'she was a very careful and loving mother', or words to that effect. Perhaps she thought she was, but William was 'her darling', and the words which Folkes's witnesses put into poor James's mouth about his fear of his mother have the ring of truth about them. Henry Wynne's evidence is particularly telling; it was he who reported that James blamed his sickness on 'his mother's unkindness to him', and Wynne, though he swore for Folkes, produced some quite damaging evidence about his deals.

Folkes probably had plotted to steal the Chapman fortune, but, it seems, he was only able to do so because of the evident antagonism between mother and son. We can only guess at what happened to the infant James at his mother's hand; all we know for certain is that he blamed her for his mental state. The nurse told the examiners at the Commons what the sinister 'keeper', Freeman, had said to her as she tidied up the dying man's room in anticipation of a visit from his mother. 'Damn her, 'tis long of her we are put to all this trouble', he said. He spoke truer than he knew.

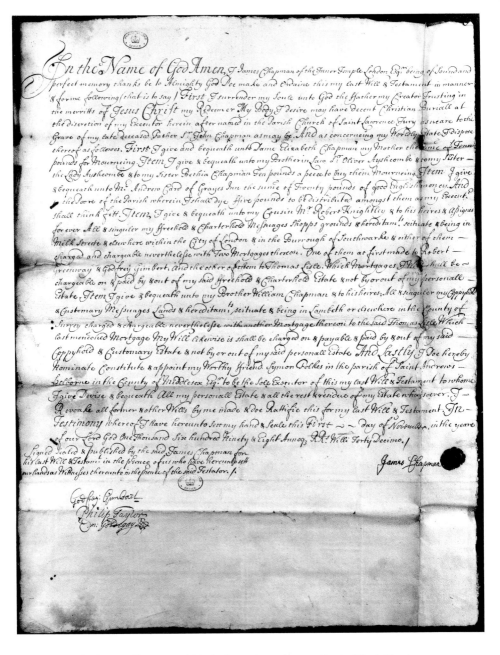

Above: The will of James Chapman, which the 'conspirators' opened in the King's Head Tavern, and (opposite): its wrapper. (Public Record Office)

'Affection defying the power of death'

Our guide on this journey has been the Devil, but before we leave the ghosts of the courts Christian, let us go briefly with Another. Happiness leaves little trace in history, but for every warring husband and wife there were hundreds who jogged along in companionable devotion. For every pair of fighting neighbours there were a thousand who exchanged pleasant chats and 'cups of sugar'. For every spiteful will there were many, many testaments of love.

The volumes of depositions kept at 6 Knightrider Street are books of hatred, but the great will registers, which represent the feelings of an infinitely greater number of souls, speak repeatedly of caring responsibility, loyalty, charity and proper affection. 'All that I have I give thee and am sorry that it is no more', writes the dying man to his wife. Overwhelmingly, testators left their worldly goods to 'loving wives and children'. All was not wrong within the families of England. Let us look at just one suit which shows how the power of parental love, assisted by the Civilians, might overcome the letter of the law and the wiles of the Devil.

In the year of the Great Frost, 1684, when the Thames was frozen over so hard that fairs were held on the ice, while the goodwives of Wapping Wall rubbed their chapped hands and the watermen were praying for a thaw, Dr Ralph Hicks, who we have just met prodding the lunatic in Broad Street, went courting in Whitechapel. The lady in question was young and rich. Elizabeth Boulter, or Betty as she was known, was the only child of a sober and solid Presbyterian couple, William and Elizabeth Boulter. Her father was a clerk in Sir Christopher Wren's office. There may have been other children, but Betty was the only one to reach adulthood, and her parents watched over her with protective love. So 'tender and fearful', were they of her that they would 'hardly suffer her out of their sight', except when she went to her dancing lessons.

Hicks was a good match, or so it seemed. He was a Yorkshireman of thirty-four with degrees from Oxford and Cambridge, an established physician with a brother who was the incumbent at All Hallows, Barking. The wedding was conducted by his brother and the couple went off to Portsmouth where Hicks had bought a practice.

In the first flush of marriage Betty wrote home to her father 'though she had not marryed the Richest Man in Hampshire . . . yet in truth she had marryed as good and as honest a Man and as tender and good a husband in having . . . Dr Hicks'. She soon changed her mind. Assuredly he was not the richest man in Hampshire, he 'never bought her a row of pins', her portion of £800 had paid for the house and practice in Portsmouth, her father had paid off debts contracted by Hicks before the marriage and met all their housekeeping bills. It was even alleged that William Boulter had bought his son-in-law's wedding outfit. Ralph Hicks was mean and bad tempered and the neighbours were soon to hear the sounds of marital discord.

There was an age gap of eighteen years and the sixteen-year-old Betty, who was used to having anything that an adoring father could provide, found life dull, confined and miserable. There were rows and scenes, and knives were thrown at the dinner-table. But Portsmouth society offered some diversions and, like many girls before and after her, she liked a 'uniform'.

In the summer of 1685, when the Hicks had been married just a year, the Duke of Norfolk's regiment, raised to put down Monmouth's Rebellion, arrived in the town, with all the clatter and glamour of flashing swords and strong young muscles. Now there were plenty of supper parties and other entertainment which brought Betty into more exciting company than she found at home. At one such party she met a handsome Irish ensign called Miles Bourke.

For the first time, one suspects, Betty Hicks fell in love. With the careless disregard of those caught up in the whirlwind of passion the couple conducted a near-public affair, which was soon the talk of Portsmouth. They made love in stables, in haylofts and the outhouses of the Hicks establishment. Mistress Boulter came down from London to try and put an end to her daughter's disgraceful behaviour. The desperate mother, according to a neighbour, would wring her hands and 'seemed ready to breake her heart and proclaimed . . . that her daughter was a whore'. Her mission was unsuccessful and uncomfortable; she had been put in a cold bedroom and caught a chill which later turned to something more serious.

Hicks decided the only way he could keep his wife (and her money?) was to remove her from Portsmouth. Some said that the profitable arrangement he had with a local apothecary had terminated, and that was the occasion of his departure. For whichever reason, he returned to London and took a house on Tower Hill, just near the church where, only two years before, Betty and he had exchanged their vows. The marriage staggered on for a little over a year. Miles had followed them to town and was caught hiding in cupboards and in the cellar of the house. The affair was a matter of 'public fame' in London now and the gallant ensign was anxious that Hicks might become violent towards his wife. He asked for an interview with the doctor and threatened him with a duel if Betty was harmed: 'If you abuse or reflect upon Mistress Hicks, your wife, on my account, I shall demand satisfaction'.

One October day in 1687 the doctor, rootling around in his wife's chamber, found a cedarwood box. He opened it up and discovered a bundle of love letters. What happened next is not revealed, but no doubt there was a final confrontation between the couple, with bitter recriminations on both sides. At all events, Betty fled to her parents' home. She did not have far to go as they now lived in a house which was safely enclosed by the great curtain walls of the Tower of London.

The Boulters took her in; many parents would have packed her off back to her husband. They were both in despair. An elderly servant said that, when he went to visit his old master, William Boulter would have tears in his eyes whenever he spoke of his daughter. As for her mother 'the same was the heart breaking of the said Elizabeth'. Miles continued to pay clandestine visits to his mistress after the parents were asleep. One night Elizabeth Boulter found him hiding under Betty's bed and chased him off, pelting him with stones.

The distress of it all took its toll and Elizabeth Boulter became ill and died of 'rheumatism and gout in her stomach'. With her mother gone, Betty took the plunge and embarked upon a new life with Miles.

It was a far cry from her old, comfortable existence and one can only hope that there was passion and fun enough between them in their bare garrets to compensate. Miles appears to have left the army and they were dependent on what Betty earned 'painting small pictures'. They moved from lodging to lodging, in the most insalubrious parts of London, perhaps avoiding creditors. In the twenty years they were together they lived in eleven different places, in a milliner's house by the Rose tavern in Covent Garden, over the shop of a fat cheesemonger, in a Quaker lodging house next to Somerset House. One baby after another arrived; most died within days of their baptism. The family ended up in a grim spot called Ship Court, just near the Old Bailey, with Miles in and out of the debtors' prison nearby.

William Boulter died without leaving a will in 1708. What had happened between him and his daughter in the preceding years is a mystery. Did Betty cut herself off completely and struggle on alone? Maybe her father tried to find her; perhaps he did, and gave her the odd guinea. Or was he too hurt? He had never liked Ralph Hicks, and was the first to admit that, but not only was Miles a bounder, he was a Roman Catholic. For a Nonconformist Protestant, living in the days of Pope burnings and all the horrors of the Popish Plot, a Catholic taken into the family in a regular way would have been abhorrent enough. What could be worse than having one's daughter run off with one of the Irish rabble that James II had rustled up in support of his wicked schemes to reinstate the Pope in England?

Ironically, it was Miles's Catholicism which was the greatest asset that Betty had when she went to the Commons to try and get her father's money away from Ralph Hicks. The old man was hardly cold in his grave when the doctor had applied for, and got, a grant of administration in the estate of his father-in-law. Betty and Miles concocted a story which, if accepted, would mean an end to their financial troubles. That it was concocted is not proven, but, even after three hundred years, the evidence produced by the Bourkes' witnesses is transparent.

When Betty was very young, before she ever met Hicks, they claimed, she had married Miles Bourke. Anticipating parental objections, on the grounds of his religion, character, etc., they kept the arrangement secret and were married privately in the Spanish Ambassador's chapel in Wild Street. Two people witnessed the event, a fourteen-year-old relative of Miles's and a mysterious flaxen-haired gentleman. In the anti-popery riots at the time of the Glorious Revolution, the chapel was burned down and its registers conveniently lost.

After the wedding Betty went back to live with her parents, or so she said, and nothing was revealed. Miles went off with the army to France. After an unspecified length of time he fell sick whilst his regiment was at Abbeville, and, thinking himself to be dying, he sent a purse of gold and his watch back to his wife in Whitechapel. When Betty received them and then heard no more she assumed he was dead. She remained convinced of that until she met him 'again', quite by chance at the fateful Portsmouth supper party.

It is difficult to imagine that the judges at the Commons swallowed this tale. They went into the matter very thoroughly; twenty-nine witnesses were examined and, at the end of it all, the decision was made, surprisingly, in Betty's favour. In all equity, the Boulter money should have been hers, but as far as the letter of the law was concerned, Hicks had a good claim. Her father's love had defied the powers of death, with the Civilians pushing from behind.

With what whoops of joy did the couple go back to their humble room in Ship Court? One hopes that they had one very good year. There appears in the Administration Act Book for 1711 a sad, stark entry: a grant of administration in the goods of William Boulter, deceased, was made to his son-in-law, Miles Bourke, his daughter and administratrix having died without administering. By April of the following year Miles too was dead.

Postscript

Our unpardonable intrusion into the private anguish of our ancestors is over. It has been a depressing trip, with no laughter, so we will make our last farewell to the 'monkish sort of attorneys' and their clients by paying a couple of short visits to lighten the atmosphere.

It is autumn in the year 1701. The most notorious of Restoration rakes, Sir Charles Sedley, the man who got Charles II drunk, and shocked even Samuel Pepys, is dying in his country mansion, St Cleere, in the village of Ightham, Kent.

Nothing particularly apposite to a tale of man's inhumanity to man arose from his death or the disposition of his property, but the account of his last hours, which has been buried away in the archives of the Prerogative for so long, serves as a *memento mori*.

Consider Sir Charles Sedley as he was in 1663, a fine, young Cavalier poet, dazzling Whitehall and exciting London society with his wit and vibrant vulgarity. At Oxford Kate's, a cook shop in Covent Garden, he stood naked on the balcony in open day light, and, 'acting all the postures of lust and buggery', shouted out that he had a powder for sale which would get all the cunts in the town after him. That cost him a debauchery fine of £500.

Now he is in his early sixties and his high living has taken its toll. Drane Farm is mortgaged and the income from his estates, exactly the sum he paid for his debauchery all those years ago, is insufficient to pay his 'book debts'.

He was taken ill in a nearby town a week ago and has been in bed with a fever ever since. Many friends are dropping in to pay their respects; he is still popular. All his life he has been a heavy brandy drinker and at the moment he is drunk or delirious much of the time, putting 'the chamberpott to his stomach and to his mouth' and imagining that the ruffled linen coverlet beneath him was a slug. 'What do those Doggs and Catts doe there, they are playing or fighting', he called out to his nurses. Charming to the last, when his childhood friend, William Maddox, comes to visit and asks how he does, Sedley, at once, asks him how *he* does.

He knows full well this is the end, has said as much and is able to sign a will and press his ring into the soft wax. It is dark when the rector arrives with the document; he is just able to take the will in one hand and a candle in the other.

That Monday night his friend the local innkeeper sat up with him; he 'called often for syder', but the nurses would only permit what the doctor had prescribed. In the morning he died.

An unremarkable enough death. His second cousin propounded the will which benefited him, but the probate was revoked in favour of Sedley's half-brother, Reginald Peckham. Subsequently another will was registered.

Nothing singular happened but, without that bit of legal proceeding, we would never have known that Sir Charles's bawdy sense of humour was alive to the very last.

When his young clergyman friend, Samuel Atwood from Ashford, came to call the afternoon before Sedley died, Peckham asked him to take the sick man's hand and feel his pulse. Atwood said he 'did not care to touch him', giving the excuse that his own hands were cold and Sir Charles was 'in a breathing sweat'. The old man, who had only minutes before been in a high delirium, spoke clearly and perhaps with a final twinkle: 'Whom will you have a touch with?', he asked.

Finally, consider another dig at the expense of the Church, this time written down by a woman with a good strong bawdy sense of humour.

Mad Mrs Morice enjoyed a joke. She was the lady who left seventeen wills and whose personal habits caused such embarrassment to one of the witnesses who appeared in the litigation which followed her death.

As might be expected, some of the parties involved were at pains to prove she was insane. She kept coal on her sitting-room floor – a painting was made of it to prove the point and exhibited in court. She wore summer trimming to her bonnet in the winter and enjoyed a good fight in the street. Moreover, she kept a book of questionable jokes. It must have provided some light relief for the Doctors as they waded through the mountains of evidence.

Mad Mrs Morice's sitting-room, with coal piled up on the floor. This painting was presented in court as evidence of her madness. (Public Record Office)

The book is there, wrapped up in a bundle with the seventeen wills. One can imagine the coarse old woman chortling as she wrote this one down, drinking 'rummer after rummer of brandy':

> The late Bishop of Durham had a slovenly custom of keeping one of his hands in his breeches, and, being one time to bring a bill to the House of Lords for the benefit of clergymen's widows, he came with the papers in one hand, and the other, as usual, in his Breeches.
>
> 'I have something in my hand, My Lords' says he, 'For the benefit of the widows of the clergy'.
>
> Upon which the Earl of Chesterfield, interrupting him, saying: 'In which hand, My Lord?'

Glossary

Advocate	The 'barrister' of the Church courts.
Apparitor	The official who served Church court summonses.
Chancery	See Court of Chancery.
Civil Law	A system of law based on Roman law. The law administered in the Church courts was an amalgam of civil law, canon law and precedent. The lawyers who practised in the Church courts were known as Civilians.
College of Advocates	The institution to which the London Civilians (see 'Civil Law', above) belonged. Its nickname was Doctors' Commons.
Commissary Court	Court of the bishop's deputy or commissary.
Common Pleas	See Court of Common Pleas.
Commons	See Doctors' Commons.
Consistory Court	Bishop's court. The 'consistorial place' was the name given to that part of the cathedral where the court sat.
Court of Arches	Appeal court for the Church courts in the province of Canterbury. The chief judge was known as the Dean.
Court of Chancery	The chief equity court. It handled disputes over wills, marriage settlements, trusts and property.
Court of Common Pleas	Royal court of justice
Courts of Conscience	Nickname for the Church courts.
Curation proxy	Authorisation for a proctor to effect the appointment of a guardian for an executor, administrator or legatee who was under age.
Doctors' Commons	Nickname for the College of Advocates (see above).
Dower	A widow's entitlement to a proportion of her husband's estate.
Equity	See Court of Chancery.
Free bench, rights of	A widow's entitlement to live in the matrimonial home after her husband's death.
Grant of administration	A grant made to the widow or next-of-kin of someone who died without leaving a will.
High Court of Admiralty	The court in Doctors' Commons which dealt with maritime disputes.
High Court of Delegates	Court of ecclesiastical appeal for the whole country, second only to the House of Lords.
Inventory and account	Suits in inventory and account might be brought in the Church courts to force the executor or administrator of

	an estate to reveal the extent of the assets. The inventory listed the deceased's belongings and the account itemised the costs incurred in the winding up of the estate.
King's Bench	Royal court of justice, administering criminal and civil law.
Nuncupative will	An unsigned note of a dying man's wishes, dictated to or overheard by witnesses.
Portion bonds	Securities for the legal distribution of estates. Entered into by administrators of intestate estates during the Interregnum.
Prerogative Court of Canterbury (PCC)	The senior court for the proving of wills in the Province of Canterbury. It sat in London. Dissolved in 1858.
Proctor	The Church courts' equivalent of a solicitor.
Scrivener	Professional 'writer' used to draw up legal documents and write letters etc. for the illiterate.
Statute of Distributions	Act passed during Charles II's reign which regulated the disposal of intestate estates.
Strict settlement	Legal arrangement made for the descent of landed property within a family.

Bibliography

The material for this book is taken almost entirely from manuscripts, some of which have only recently become available for research.

A detailed study of probate procedure and the Prerogative Court of Canterbury is in preparation by the author. In the meantime, a provisional guide is available: Jane Cox, *Wills, Inventories and Death Duties* (Public Record Office, 1988).

Introduction

The novels by Charles Dickens that contain references to the Commons are:

> *Pickwick Papers* (1836–1837)
>
> *Sketches by Boz* (1836–1837)
>
> *David Copperfield* (1849–1850)
>
> *Our Mutual Friend* (1864–1865).

See also Walter Dexter, 'Roundabout the Commons', *The Dickensian* 27 (1931). The transcriptions made in court by Dickens himself are in the Guildhall Library (*Jarman v Bagster*, MS 20, 778).

1 Setting the Scene

The official records of the institution known as Doctors' Commons are in Lambeth Palace Library. The records of the courts which sat there, however, are scattered as follows:

> The Court of Arches – Lambeth Palace Library
>
> The High Court of Delegates – Public Record Office
>
> The High Court of Admiralty – Public Record Office
>
> The Prerogative Court of Canterbury – Public Record Office
>
> The Bishop of London's Consistory Court – Greater London Record Office
>
> The Bishop of London's Commissary Court – Guildhall Library
>
> The Archdeacon of London's Court – Guildhall Library.

The picture of the Commons and the Prerogative Office in the 1830s was written after consulting the following:

> The records of the Prerogative Court of Canterbury in the Public Record Office, mainly the correspondence of officials in the class PROB 39 and material as yet unclassified

The Dickens novels cited above

G D Squibb, *Doctors' Commons* (London, 1977)

The *Post Office Directories* for London

The *Law List*

4th Report of the Commissioners of Inquiry into the Law of England respecting Real Property, Appendix 1833 (226) XXII.1 (London, 1833)

Royal Commission to inquire into Process, Practice and Systems of Pleading in the Court of Chancery, 2nd report, Minutes of Evidence, Appendix 1854 (1731) XXIV.1 (London, 1854)

'Turkey Quill', 'Doctors' Commons in the seventies', *Red Tape,* October 1924

E J Pickard and E Jeffries Davies, 'The rebuilding of the Commons, 1666–1672'; E Jeffries Davies, 'Doctors' Commons, the late history of the property', *London Topographical Record,* XV (1931)

L W Cowie, 'Doctors' Commons', *History Today* (June 1970)

J Conway Davies, 'Report on the Records of the PCC', Public Record Office report (unpublished), 1964.

The history of the courts and the procedure therein is taken from a great number of printed and manuscript sources, largely culled from a lifetime spent working in the Prerogative Court records. The most useful published manuals are:

R Burn, *The Ecclesiastical Law,* corrected by Phillimore (London, 1842)

A Brown, *A Compendious View of the Civil Law* (Dublin, 1799)

J Godolphin, *The Orphans' Legacy* (London, 1701)

The Law of Testaments (London, 1744)

R Newcourt, *Repertorium Ecclesiasticum* (London, 1708)

H Swinburne, *A Brief Treatise of Testaments and Last Wills* (London, 1611)

T Wentworth, *The Office and Duty of Executors* (London, 1829).

Witham Friary church is described in M McGarvie, *Witham Friary Church and Parish* (Frome, 1989).

The reference to the baby who said 'fast and pray' is from *Wriothesley's Chronicle,* Camden Society (London, 1878), vol II, the entry is dated 19 May 1555.

The attack on the bishops' courts is in Edward Whitaker's pamphlet *The Bishops' Courts Dissolved* (1681) (British Library).

Dr Johnson is quoted in the *Law Times,* 2 July 1938.

The records of the Ruskin nullity case are in the Guildhall Library, MS 11, 930.

For the end of the Commons, see:

The Times, 7 February 1848

Punch, 6 June and 12 December 1857

Illustrated London News, 4 May 1867

Public Record Office, PROB 37/1781.

The examples of 'bold Restoration women' are taken from PCC Depositions (PROB 24/6) and Cause Papers (Sarah Lambeth, PROB 28/2).

2 At the Court of Marriage

Studies of marriage litigation in the Arches and the Consistory Court have been made by Lawrence Stone in *The Road to Divorce* (Oxford, 1990).

Specific references to cases reported in the text are as follows:

Domestic violence in seventeenth-century London

(Charles and Mary Pepys) *Pepys v Pepys,* London Consistory Court, Act Book DLC 35, and Depositions, DLC 242 (Greater London Record Office); Edwin Chappell, *Eight Generations of the Pepys Family* (Blackheath, 1936).

An eighteenth-century society divorce

(Stoney Bowes and the Countess of Strathmore) *Bowes v Bowes,* London Consistory Court, Allegations and Sentences, DLC 180, and Depositions, DLC 282 (Greater London Record Office); Lady Strathmore's scrap-book (private collection); Jessé Foot, *The Lives of Andrew Robinson Bowes Esq. and the Countess of Strathmore* (London, 1820).

3 At the Court of Scolds

Studies of the subject which have been consulted include:

Christopher Hill, *A Turbulent, Seditious and Factious People* (Oxford, 1988)

M J Ingram, *Church Courts, Sex and Marriage in England, 1540–1640* (Cambridge, 1987)

L A Knafla, ' "Sin of all sorts swarmeth", criminal litigation in an English county in the early seventeenth century', in *Law, Litigants and the Legal Profession,* Royal Historical Society Studies in History no. 36, ed. E W Ives and A H Manchester (London, 1983)

J A Sharpe, *Defamation and Slander in Early Modern England, the Church Courts at York,* Borthwick Papers no. 58 (York, 1981)

J A Sharpe, ' "Such Disagreement btwyxt Neighbours", Litigation and Human Relations in Early Modern England', in *Disputes and Settlements,* ed. J Bossy (Cambridge, 1983)

G R Quaife, *Wanton Wenches and Wayward Wives* (London, 1979)

D E Underdown, 'The taming of the scold: the enforcement of patriarchal authority in early modern England' in *Order and Disorder in Early Modern England,* ed. A Fletcher and J Stevenson (Cambridge, 1985)

R M Wunderli, *London Church Courts and Society on the Eve of the Reformation* (Cambridge, Massachusetts, 1981)

Richard Gough, *The History of Myddle,* ed. P Razell (London, 1979).

The general London background can be found in the following works:

The London Encyclopaedia, ed. B Weinreb and C Hibbert (London, 1983)

London 1500–1700: The Making of the Metropolis, ed. A L Beier and R Finlay (London, 1986)

The A to Z of Elizabethan London, ed. A Prockter, R Taylor and J Fisher (London, 1979)

F C Chalfant, *Ben Jonson's London* (Athens, Georgia, 1978)

John Stow's Survey of London, 1598, ed. J Wheatley (London, 1987)

V Pearl, *London and the Outbreak of the Puritan Revolution* (Oxford, 1961)

T F Reddaway, *The Rebuilding of London after the Great Fire* (London, 1940)

T Harris, *London Crowds in the Reign of Charles II* (London, 1987)

The Diary of Samuel Pepys ed. R Latham and W Matthews (London, 1970–1983)

M Dorothy George, *London Life in the Eighteenth Century* (London, 1925)

W J Pike, *History of Clerkenwell* (London, 1881)

E Beresford Chancellor, *The Annals of Fleet Street* (London, 1912)

W G Bell, *Fleet Street through Seven Centuries* (London, 1912).

Much of the information about East London comes from the author's researches for her forthcoming book on the area, provisionally titled *London's Backyard.*

Sources for the general discussion of 'neighbours in slander actions' include:

Ben Jonson, *The Devil is an Ass* (1616)

Antimoxeia, the honest design of Tower Hamlets for the suppressing of bawdy houses, Guildhall Pamphlet (1691)

Frances Consitt, *The London Weavers' Company* (London, 1933)

William Wycherley, *The Country Wife* (1675)

(Isabella Newport) Guildhall MS 9065

(1622 proclamation against brothels) E J Burford, *London, the Synfulle Citie* (London, 1990)

C Larner, *Enemies of God* (London, 1981)

(Joan Haughton) *Haughton v Harrow,* Guildhall MS 9189/2.

References and works relating to specific lawsuits cited in the next sections of this chapter are as follows:

At the court of the Archdeacon of London in Elizabethan times

Archdeaconry Court Depositions, Guildhall MS 9056.

At the Bishop of London's court in the 1620s

Thomas Middleton, *The Black Book* (1604), Prologue

Ben Jonson, *Bartholomew Fair* (1614), Act I

Eaton v Hooper, etc., Commissary Court Depositions, Guildhall MS 9189/2.

The years leading to the Civil War

Bartholomew Faire (anti-Laudian tract of 1641) Guildhall Pamphlet AN 6.4, no 1 in 32 (facsimile, c. 1868)

G Huelin, *William Laud and the Church in London,* Guildhall Pamphlet 2343 (1973)

(the prosecutions of 1634–6) Guildhall MSS 9051/1 and 2, 9274

(the Archdeaconry cases) Depositions, Guildhall MS 9057/1.

In Nell Gwynne's day

The Night Walker or Evening Rambles in search after lewd women (1696, reprinted London, 1970)

(cases in the Consistory) *Ford v Shelley, Field v Holgate, Holgate v Richman, Healey v Bentley, Wells v Mitchell, Winterbottom v Burton)* Depositions, DLC 240, Sentences, DLC 143, Act Book, DLC 34 (Greater London Record Office).

4 At the Court of Death

The source for probate procedure is the whole range of Prerogative Court records and the manuals and other works listed for chapter 1, 'Setting the Scene'. Of particular value are the reports of the Commissions on Chancery and Real Property. Specific references are as follows (they are mostly to Prerogative Court of Canterbury records held in the Public Record Office under the lettercode PROB):

William Hayward dec., PROB 31/734/820

(Humphrey Bawden) *Gannacliffe v Munckley,* PROB 28/1031 B

(James Pilgrim Warner) *Warner v Warner,* PROB 18 for 1801

(the Earl of Anglesey) *Haversham & Anglesey v the Countess of Anglesey,* PROB 18/27

(the suicidal herald) *John Hare dec., Bedingfield v Hare,* PROB 24/54; PROB 18/35

(Nell Gwynne) Jane Hoare, 'The death of Nell Gwynne', *History Today* (June 1977)

(Sir Thomas Woolryche) *Swale v Woolrich alias Hewley* (1662) PROB 24/4

Elizabeth Morice dec., PROB 37/813; PROB 26/69 and 70; PROB 18/125

(Maria Lumsden) PROB 27 (4 July 1661)

Streete v Streete, PROB 18/3/36

Cinderella

(George Carteret) PROB 19/1

(John Jacob Vesenbeck) PROB 10/1736 (will) and PROB 11/635 s 23

Portion bonds, Exchequer, E 315/483 f.68 (1654)

(Sir Leoline Jenkins and the Statute of Distributions) J Cox 'Sir Leoline Jenkins', University of London MPhil dissertation (unpublished), 1973; W Wynne, *The Life of Sir Leoline Jenkins* (London, 1724)

(the cat on the malt heap) Thomas Wilson, 'The State of England Anno Domini 1600', ed. F J Fisher, *Camden Miscellany,* XVI, 3rd series, 52 (1936)

John Baker dec., Bateman v Hibbins, PROB 24/6

Roger Faucus dec., Bull v Clarke alias Faucus, PROB 18/26/149 and PROB 24/39

(Johanne Bewes) *Goutier alias Bewes v Bewes,* correspondence of the proctor, Francis Boycott (1737), PROB 39

(Tobias Wyseman) *Wyseman v Wyseman* (1670), PROB 16/4

(John Hitson) *Ralph Barnes dec.* (1670), PROB 32/8, grant of administration (1658), PROB 6/34.

Gold-diggers and good-time girls

(Lucy Hungate abducts a girl) *Wray v Wray,* PROB 47 (1679–81)

('In Oliver's day') *Parry v Smith,* PROB 28/557 (1703)

(Lucy Hungate and Sir Chichester Wray) *Wray v Wray,* PROB 47 (1679–81); proceedings in the Court of Delegates, DEL 3/15; Chancery (1707), C 7/211/29; *Lee v Wray,* Consistory proceedings, DLC 34.

(John Moore 'of weak parts') *Gilliver alias Moore v Hand,* PROB 47 (1706)

(Old Weedon of Bosmear) *Weedon v Weedon,* PROB 28/1212; PROB 18/27; will, PROB 11/477 s 158; Chancery, C 7/264/2.

Fathers

John Milton, *Lives of the English Poets,* ed. G B Hill (first published 1905, reprinted New York 1967); PROB 20/1817, PROB 24/13, PROB 29/57

(Sir John Soane) Soane MSS at the Soane Museum; Pierre de la Ruffinière, *John Soane's Architectural Education* (London, 1977); PROB 37/1062; Chancery, C 33/888–909.

Mothers

H Crichton Miller, *The New Psychology and the Parent* (London, 1922)

(The widow Dewes) PROB 28/794

(Abraham Rookes) *Dedeuxville v Deane,* PROB 24/8; PROB 5/2750; PROB 18/3; PROB 28/117

(Mary Martin) *Allured v Allured,* PROB 18/3; PROB 29/54; PROB 24/8; PROB 5/2377

(Lady Chapman and her son James) *Folkes v Chapman,* PROB 24/38 and 40; PROB 18/25; will of Sir John Chapman, PROB 11/395 s 60; will of James Chapman, PROB 20/469; *Dr John Scott, A Sermon Preached at the Funeral of Sir John Chapman, 27 March, 1689,* Guildhall Pamphlet; R R Sharpe, *London and the Kingdom* (London, 1894).

'Affection defying the power of death'

(Ralph Hicks and Betty Boulter) *Bourke v Hicks, William Boulter dec.,* PROB 28/711; PROB 24/48 and 49; PROB 6/87; William Munk, *Roll of the Royal College of Physicians* (London, 1878).

Postscript

Reference to specific cases are as follows:

Sir Charles Sedley dec., Tomlyn v Peckham, PROB 11/461 s 118; PROB 11/463 s 40, PROB 24/40; Pepys's diary, 1 July 1663 (*The Diary of Samuel Pepys* ed. R Latham and W Matthews (London, 1970–1983)).

Elizabeth Morice dec., PROB 37/813.